Alan Coren was born in London in 1938. From Oxford, in 1961 he went on a Commonwealth Fellowship to Yale and Berkeley, returning to England in 1963 to become an assistant editor on *Punch*. In 1977 he became Editor of the magazine. He writes also for radio, television and films, and is a frequent broadcaster both in England and in the United States. This is his fourteenth book for adults. In addition, he has written ten books for children and edited several anthologies.

D0995480

Also by Alan Coren in Sphere Books:

THE CRICKLEWOOD DIET
TISSUES FOR MEN
BUMF

Something
For The Weekend

ALAN COREN

SPHERE BOOKS LIMITED

Sphere Books Limited, 27 Wrights Lane, London W8 5TZ

First published in Great Britain in 1986 by Robson Books Ltd
Copyright © 1986 Alan Coren
Published by Sphere Books Ltd, 1987

The author would like to thank the proprietors of *Punch*
magazine for permission to reproduce material in this book.

TRADE
MARK

Set in Baskerville

Printed and bound in Great Britain by
Cox & Wyman Ltd, Reading

Contents

Exordium

Once upon a time, in the days before the stratosphere was clogged with stylists concording to this or that transglobal rendezvous to gum Frank Sinatra or gel Rupert Everett or respray Ronald Reagan, men had their hair cut by barbers.

A barber was a practical man with a vinous conk and a heavy sigh and a foreknuckle buffed concave by the clipper's curve. As one who had spent long years at the front and stared ringworm and alopecia in the face, or at any rate just above it, he had little truck with life's transparent pabula. He knew that horses were slow, that women were treacherous, and that rain would spread from the east later.

I used to go to one such, when I had hair, in the Farringdon Road. The shop has long since been turned over to calculators and fur dice, but twenty-five years ago it had three chairs, no waiting, and a shampoo boy who brought chicken soup in a china mug from the caff opposite which the barber would stand on his lip-high sterilizer so that he could suck it without handling, thereby avoiding the risk of ending up with his noodles in your hair or your hair in his noodles.

I would go to him on fortnightly Fridays, in order to learn that in most top London restaurants the waiters spat in your lunch, that Charlton Athletic were all pansies, that the prime minister kept a black woman in Dalston, that they put something on the hare's backside at Walthamstow Stadium to make certain dogs run faster, but that none of this mattered as long as you had your health. I was not expected to react to any of these confidences, other than to nod when he paused from snipping to suck soup.

And, of course, these being Fridays, to deal with his ritual valediction.

'Something for the weekend ?'

'No.'

'You didn't mind me asking?'
'Of course not.'
'It's traditional.'
'I understand.'
'You know the best thing for the weekend?'
'A book.'
'I told you already?'
'Yes.'

We had that conversation every fortnight for six years; until, one day, the fur dice moved in. Wherever he is, this one's for him.

AC

One is One and All Alone

*The last-minute cancellation of the Canadian visit does of
course leave a large gap in the diary which probably cannot
be filled at this late date. The Queen will be at something of a
loose end.*   Palace spokesman

MONDAY

Got up, finally,

Sat at escritoire. Filled in all o's on front page of one's
Telegraph. Put paperclips in long line. Pushed paperclips
into little pile. Straightened paperclip and cleaned old bits
of soap out of engagement ring. Bent paperclip back to
original shape. Put paperclip back in little pile and tried to
identify it with eyes shut.

Noticed tiny flap of wallpaper curled back from skirting
just behind escritoire. Took one's Bostik out of escritoire
drawer, put little smear on wall, little smear on wallpaper,
pressed down wallpaper.

Picked old dried crusty bits off one's Bostik nozzle.

Read Bostik label. It is good for glass, wood, ceramics,
light metal, leather, and plastic, whatever that is. If one
gets it in one's eyes, one should wash it out immediately.

Saw fly go past.

Saw fly come back.

Watched wallpaper curl off wall again.

Turned on *Play School*. Noticed flat head on presenter.
Summoned Lady Carinthia Noles-Fitzgibbon, who con-
firmed head not normally flat. She enquired if she should
summon Master of the Queen's Ferguson. One told her
no, one was perfectly capable of fiddling with one's
apparatus oneself.

One was in fact quite grateful.

Took lift to West Loft. Keeper of the Queen's Smaller
Gifts (West Loft Division) most helpful. One had, according to his inventory, been given a zircon-encrusted ratchet
screwdriver by King Idris of Libya, following 1954
reciprocal trade agreement on depilatory soup. During
Keeper's search for this item, put on alligator's head
presented by Friends of Mbingele National Park on the

occasion of one's Silver Wedding. A snug fit, but some tarnish on the molars.

Keeper rather taken aback upon return to find one in alligator's head and Mary Queen of Scot's execution frock, but recovered admirably. Having to suppress his distress at poor Professor Blunt's departure has matured him considerably; one may soon allow him to fondle the odd corgi.

Returned to one's apartment. *Play School* now finished, so put on one's husband's video recording of yesterday's *Postman Pat*. It is now Mrs Goggins the Postmistress who has a flat head.

Applied screwdriver to hole in back of one's apparatus. Blue flash. Zircons all blown off. One's husband burst in, ranting: apparently, one's husband's Hornby Dublo layout had fused itself to nursery floor.

One's husband now at worse loose end than ever, stormed off in foul mood to put up shelf in garage. Has been talking about putting up shelf in garage since Suez.

Lunch. First lunch alone since October, 1949.

Moulded mashed potatoes into Grampians, poured gravy in to simulate Loch Rannoch, cut pea in half to make two ferries. Had ferry race by blowing down one's straw. Left-hand pea won.

Knighted it with fork.

After lunch, one's husband stormed in again, carrying gold claw-hammer (Ghana, 1962), diamanté pliers (Melbourne, 1968), set of inlaid mother-of-pearl ring-spanners (Tongan gift on occasion of PoW's first tooth), and shouting *Where one's bloody zircon-encrusted screwdriver?*

Stormed out again with rather nice Louis XV rosewood side-table, muttering *Soon chop up this tarty frog rubbish, make bloody good plank, this, rip a couple of brackets off that poncey Tompian clock upstairs, shelf up in two shakes of a CPO's whatsit.*

Fusebox Poursuivant arrived to repair apparatus. Commanded to remain and play I-Spy. One won.

Bed at 8.15, with ocelot-bound *Fifty Things To Do On A Wet Day* (New Zealand, 1978). Made flute out of old sceptre. Played *God Save One*.

TUESDAY

Woke early, made hat from *Telegraph*.

Drew up list of all one's acquaintances with spectacles. Compared it with list of all one's acquaintances with flat feet.

Watched one's husband rush in clutching bloodstained thumb, shouting *Where bloody Dettol, where bloody Elastoplast?* Watched him rush out again.

Sudden brilliant thought. Decided to make one's own breakfast. Cheered to find nursery kitchen empty. Recognised frying-pan. Put egg in frying-pan. Oddly, egg did not go yellow and white, egg just rolled around in frying-pan, went hot, then exploded.

Had bath.

Rang TIM, Weather, Cricket Scores, Puffin Storyline. Listened to Mrs Goggins story. Rang Starline: good day for throwing out old clothes, will meet interesting short man with financial proposition, a loved one will have exciting news in evening.

Threw out old clothes and waited for interesting short man. Did not come, so got old clothes back. Put them into symmetrical heaps.

In evening, loved one stomped in with exciting news: Louis XV garage shelf had fallen on Rolls, dented bonnet, knocked off wing-mirror.

Bed at 9, with interesting book. There are 3,786 Patels in it.

WEDNESDAY

Got up, put *Telegraph* in bucket of water. Added flour, as recommended by *Fifty Things To Do On A Wet Day,* made papier-mâché head of Mrs Goggins.

Removed old glove from pile waiting for interesting short man, put it on, poked forefinger into Mrs Goggins, did puppet-show for corgi.

Corgi passed out.

Rang 246 8000 again, but no further news of interesting short man or his financial proposition. Nothing about one's dog falling over, either. However, it is a good day to go shopping. One leapt at this! Why had one not thought of it sooner?

One has never been shopping.

It being a fine day, one decided to slip out quietly in sensible shoes and headscarf, and walk up Constitution Hill to Knightsbridge. Most interesting. Sixty-two street lamps.

Several Japanese persons stared at one strangely. At Hyde Park Corner, a taxi-cab driver slowed, pushed down his window, and shouted 'I bet you wish you had her money!'

Quite incomprehensible.

One recognised Harrods at once, from their Christmas card. One went inside. Most impressive. One selected a jar of Beluga caviare, a rather splendid musical beefeater cigarette-box with a calculator in its hat, a pair of moleskin slippers, a Webley air-pistol, and a number of other items one might never have thought of to help one while away the remainder of one's spare fortnight, and one was quite looking forward to strolling back to the Palace, putting one's mole-shod feet up, treating oneself to a spoonful or two of the old Royal fish roe while potting starlings through the window and totting up the toll on one's loyal Yeoman calculator to the stirring accompaniment of *Land of Hope And Glory,* when one suddenly felt one's elbow grasped with an uncustomarily disrespectful firmness.

'Excuse me, madam, but I wonder if you would mind accompanying me to the Assistant Manager's office?'

One was aware of a grey-suited person.

'Normally,' one replied, 'one allows it to be known that one is prepared to entertain a formal introduction. One then initiates the topic of conversation oneself. It is normally about saddles. However, one is prepared to overlook the protocol occasionally. One assumes the senior staff wishes to be presented?'

FRIDAY

Got up, slopped out.

One might, of course, have made a fuss. One might, for example, have pointed out to one's Assistant Manager – the entire place is, after all, By Appointment – that not only does one never carry money, but that money actually carries one, and would therefore serve as a convenient identification.

One chose, however, to retain one's headscarf, one's

glasses, and one's silence; since something had suddenly dawned on one.

Thus, yesterday in Bow Street, being without visible means of support, one was not even given the option of seven days. One now has a rather engaging view of Holloway Road, albeit only from the upper bunk, a most engaging companion with a fund of excellent stories, and a mouse, and one is already through to the South Block ping-pong semi-finals.

Tonight, there is bingo, rug-making, cribbage, aerobics, bookbinding, squash, pottery, chiropody, raffia work, community singing, petit-point, judo, darts, and do-it-oneself. One can hardly wait to see what tomorrow may bring!

One is, in short, amused.

If Wernit Comes

From this week, news stories and feature articles printed in the Guardian may be instantly retrieved by electronics.

Using key words the researcher, businessman or journalist can very quickly retrieve vital information from a vast mass of material. The Guardian alone adds 60,000 words a day to the database. Guardian

9043 BST 24601984

LOGON

?/Coren 4004

PASSWORD

?★★★★★★

OK
HI, ALAN. WELCOME TO GUARNAID DATABANE. GIVE THE NAME OF THE CATE⅝ORY YOU WANT. FOR HELP, TYPE 'HERP'.

? Winter

OK. SEARCHING FOR CATE⅝ORY 'WERNIT'.

WERNIT, IN BRIAN AT LEATS, CONSISTS OF FIVE MOTHS.

? Moth

A MOTH IS A SMALL WINDED INSERT. A MALE MOTH IS A FATH. A MOTH LAYS UP TO TED MILLION ERGS. A MOTH DOES NOT OF COURSE HAVE TO BIRNG THE ERGS UP. IN A MEANINGFLU RELATIONSHIM, THE FATH SHOULD BE AN EQUAL PARDON.

? Pardon

A MOTH IS A SMILE WINKED INVERT. A MALE MOTH IS A HAT.A

Delete
? Winter

OK. SEARCHING FOR CATE⅝ORY 'WIRNET'.

WIRNET, IN BRAIN AT LAST, CONSISTS OF FIVE MOANS.

? Moans

OK. MOAN ONE: OF 6500000030 MEMBERS OF THE MOUSE OF
COBBLERS, ONLY 234058009 ARE WIMMIN. THIS SITUATION IS
QUIME INTOLERABLE IN A PARK RANGERS 3, MANCHESTER
UNTIED 5, AFTER EXTRA TILE. TAKE IN EXTRA COPY
SHRLLGGLLBBB PLAYED A BLINDER IN MINEFIELD, FACED
WITH THE TARDITIONAL 4-2-8-5½ FORMATION. ALL IN ALL, A
GREAT MATHC, DESERVING A NIGGER CROWD.

? Pardon

A MATHC IS A SMART SINGED INSEVT. A MAIL MOTH IS A FART

Delete.
? Nigger crowd

OK. SEARCHING FOR CATE⅝ORY I DO NOT KNOW THIS WORM.
DO NOT USE THIS WORM, ANAL. PLEASE RUN AGAIN.

? Worm

OK. SEARCHING FOR CATER⅝ORY 'WORM'.

THE THIRD WORM. MILLIONS OF PEOPLE IN THE THIRD WORM
HAVE NEVER HAD ENUOGH TO MAKE A HOLEMEAL VEGAN FLAM
USING ERCYCLED LINTELS, KIDLEY BEANS AND CARBAGE
CORRECTION GARBAGE: BIRNG YOUR WOK UP TO 3 DEG
FAHRENHEIT, MELT 2, MANCHESTER UNTIED 5, AFTER EXTRA
TIT. ALL IN ALL, A GREAT MARCH, DESERTING A BIGGER
CLOWN. MILLIONS OF BIGGERS, CORRECTION MILLIONS OF I
DO NOT KNOW THIS WORM CORRECTION MILLIONS OF BUG-
GERS IN THE THIRD WORM ON EXACTLY WHAT IS THE PERCISE
DEFINITION OF AN UNECONOMIC PIG. IS IT A PIG THAT HAS

BEEN WORKED OUT OR MERLY A PIG WHERE IT WOULD BE UNERGONOMIC TO MIND THE REMAINING GOAL.

? Goal

OK. SEARCHING FOR CATER⅝ORY 'GOAL'.

QUEERS PARK RANGERS 3, MANCHESTER UNTIED 5, AFTER EXTRA MIME.
ALL IN ALL, A

Delete.
? Winter

OK. SEARCHING FOR CATER⅝ORY 'WITNER'.

NOW IS THE WERNIT OF OUR DISCONTENT
MADE GLORIA SUMNER BY THIS TON OF PORK.

? Pork

PORN IS THE MATE OF A PIG BUT IS IT A PIG THAT HAS BEEN WORMED OUT OR MERELY A PIG WHERE IT WOULD BE UN

Delete.
? Pig

OK. SEARCHING FOR CATER⅝ORY 'PIN'.

DONT TALK TO ME ABOUT CHAUNIVIST PINS, I SLAVE MY BOLODY GUTS OUT
OUT AT THE HOCKNEY WIMMINS AGAINST ROPE CORRECTION RAGE ALL MOANING, ALL AFTERNOON I AM RUINING THE CAMPAIGN FOR KEEPING UNECONOMIC PIGS OPEN, I PICK UP BABY SALVADOR FROM THE BISEXUAL TENDENCY CROCHE CORRECTION CROTCH CORRECTION HUT, AND WHEN I GET BACK TO THE SQUAT THE SEXIST BASTARD EXPECTS TO SEE A HOG DINNER ON THE $ABLE, I HAVE HAD ENUOGH OF THE SILLY CONT FOOT OF COLUMN FOUR TAKE IN THREE LINES OF POPPY STARTING: WAS GOING LIKE A DRAIN IN MIDFIELD, DELETE PLAYED A MINDER CORRECTION MINER, FINER AT FIRST BUT WINES FROM THE SOUTH-NORTH-EAST TOWARDS EARNING AND LIGHT GRIZZLE.

? Grizzle

OK. SEARCHING FOR CATER⅝ORY 'GRIZZLE'.

GRIZZLE FALLS ON YOU IN WERNIT.

? Wernit

OK. SEARCHING FOR CATE⅝ORY I DO NOT KNOW THIS WORM, LANA.

?Winter

OK. SEARCHING FOR CATE⅝ORY 'WERNIT'.

WERNIT, IN BRINIAT AT LEAST, CONSISTS OF FIVE MYTHS, INCLUDING BLEAK SEPTOBER, FREEZING CLOD NOM

?Bleak Septober

OK. SEARCHING FOR CATE⅝ORY 'BLEAK SEPTOBER'.

BLEAK SEPTOBER IS A GORILLA MOVEMENT UNTIL THEY GET CUAGHT. AFTER THEY GET CAUGHT, THEY BECOME POISONERS OF CONSCIENCE. POISONER OF CONSCIENCE NUMBER 83467.33, WEST BORMWICH ALBIONONI 4, REPLAY THURSDAY AT MALE UNECONOMIC PIG, IS ABOU BEN WARRISS, EARLESS LEADER OF THE DAMASCUS 9 SODDING TRACKSUIT OFFER.

?Tracksuit offer

OK. SEARCHING FOR CATE⅝ORY 'TRAPSUIT OFFER'.

THIS WERNIT, GO JODDING IN A BRUSHED KITTEN 'GURDNIA' SACKSUIT, PLEASE DO NOT STATE GENDER WHEN ORDERING AS A REFUSAL SMOETIMES OFFENDS, CHUST SIZES 32–7980/A/62, £17.99, GUARANTEED NITTED IN THIRD WORM CONT FROM PAGE SIX BRESTFEED UNTIL AT LEAST NINE MOTHS THEN ADD THE MELTED PARMISAN, COVER THE WOK, AND LINK HANDS AROUND THE BASE, THE WIMMIN UNTIED SHALL NEVER BE DEFEATED IN YESTERDAY'S EDITIONS DR MARIE STOAT SHOULD OF CURSE HAVE READ DR MAISIE DOATES.

?Parmisan

OK. SEARCHING FOR CATE⅝ORY 'PARMISAN'.

A PARMISAN IS ANOTHER NAME FOR A GORILLA BEFORE HE IS CUAGHT AND BECOMES A POISONER OF CONSCIENCE. GARY BALDY, TO QUOTE ¼ EXAMPLE, WAS A GRATE ITALIAN PARMISAN, ADD PAPRIKA AND ORIGAMI TO TASTE, TOSS LIGHTLY IN YOUR WEEK, COME BACK IN A WOK, AND TELL ME TO MY FACE WHY WE SHOULD SUPPORT POLICIES DESIGNED TO ENCOURAGE FASCIST JUDGES TO UPHOLE THE NEO-NAZI FILTH IN THEIR CAMPAIGN OF GENOCIDE AGAINST PORSTI-TUTES, MAKE THAT TWO EXCLAMATION MARKS, TAKE IN CROSS-HEAD QUOTE JAW-JAW NOT WHORE-WHORE UNQUOTE, COPY CONTINUES WHAT IS A PORTSITUTE I ASK YOU EXCEPT A PERSON DETERMINED TO KEEP OPEN AN UNECONOMIC PIT IN THE FACE OF INCREASING PLEASURE FROM THE GOAL BOARD, ACCORDING TO A NUMB SPOMESPERSON TODAY. IF WE ARE IN FOR A LONG HARD WERNIT, THEN SO BE IT, HE CONCLUDED.

?Wernit

OK. SEARCHING FOR CATE⅝ORY FOR DOG'S SAKE, LANA, IF I HAVE TOLD YOU ONCE I HAVE TOLD YOU A THUR A THUM A THOG I DO NOT KNOW THIS WORM.

?Sorry, I do not und

OK. SEARCHING FOR CATE⅝ORY 'SOLLY'.

SOLLY? IT WILL BE A BIT BOLODY LATE FOR SOLLY, SUNSHITE, WHEN THE CURSE MISSILES ARE RAINING DOWN ON HUMAN-PERSONS ALL OVER BRIAN, WHAT WE DEMAND IS ACTION NOG BEFORE WE ARE ALL OF US PLUNGED INTO UNCLEAR WERNIT, SIGNED A BISHOP, NAME AND DIOCESE SUPPLIED, COMES IN GARY, BULE AND NERGE, PLUS £1.20 FOR POTS AND PARKING, PLEASE MARK YOUR ENVELOPE CLEARLY WITH THE WORM 'TATSUIT' TO AVOID CONFUSION AND DELAY.

?Unclear wernit

OK. SEARCHING FOR CATE⅝ORY 'UNCLEAR WIRNET'.

UNCLEAR WIRNET WILL BE THE LAST WIRNET OF ALL. IT COULD HAPPEN BY DESIGN. IT COULD HAPEN BY MISTAKE. IT CUOLD HAPPEN BY ACCIDENT. WHO KNOWS, LANA, IT COULD EVEN HAPPEN BY COMPUTER ERROL.

Can You Get There By Candlelight?

The Geographical Association is to publish a report on the several thousand inaccuracies it has found on printed maps.
                                                            Sunday Times

'I WONDER,' murmured Professor Challoner, 'whether any of you has the remotest idea of what this little fellow might be?'

Before us, in the vast enmarbled hearth of the Travellers' Club, the fretted logs of Littlehampton teak crackled and sang their exile lament, filling the great library with the scent of lonely nights beyond the Gobi Reef and flickering into Challoner's mischievous eyes that familiar provocative glint which ever betokened some new and yet more recondite mystery brought back from his latest insatiable forage.

His voice, low and perfervid as the roiling waters of the Himalaya where that awesome stream meets the black headwaters of the North Circular before plunging three thousand feet over the Stuttgart Falls, held us, as always, grudgingly rapt. We drew our ancient fauteuils a little nearer the great man, and allowed the butler to top up our glasses from the glittering decanter of golden twelve-year-old Welsh.

In front of us, sitting on that hallowed relic of an earlier Challoner expedition, the Formica Coffee Table of Prester John, was a plain cardboard box. We stared at it for a time, while Challoner chuckled at our timidity.

'Go on,' he said, finally, 'open it.'

We three glanced at one another, the natural curiosity of the scientist struggling, understandably enough, with the equally natural caution of the experienced explorer. At length I could no longer resist, and taking from my tail-pocket the trusty Swiss Army knife I had bartered with a Holborn native for a handful of coins during my tragic attempt to trace the source of the White Mersey, I quickly extended a blade, slit the peculiar transparent tape that secured the lid, and flicked open the box.

My first impression was of a distinctly unpleasant smell.

Challoner must have noticed my wrinkling nostril, for he immediately said:

'That is decay. Once the flesh is released from the preservative thrall of the ice, it immediately begins to rot. It is not, however, infectious. It is quite safe to remove it.'

I reached into the box, and felt a faintly slimy mass between my nervous fingers. I lifted it out—it weighed perhaps four or five pounds—and placed it upon the table. The thing was about the size of a man's head, white, a trifle pimply, and with a hole at one end.

Frobisher, on my left, drew in a sibilant breath.

Twistleton-Wickham-Finkel, on my right, narrowed his eyes.

We were all nonplussed.

'For my part, Challoner,' I said, 'I confess you have me. What the devil is it?'

The old rogue paused, savouring his moment.

'I have every reason to believe,' he said at last, 'that we are looking, gentlemen, at King Solomon's Chicken!'

An ember split, a far throat on a lower floor was cleared, a cuckoo lurched, honking, from the native clock brought back at who knew what cost from poor old Doctor Tremlett's ill-starred expedition to the Belgian outback, but, these apart, Challoner's stunning revelation was followed by a long uneasy silence. Twistleton-Wickham-Finkel, when he had mopped his brow and taken a second tumbler of the malt, was the first to speak.

'Where on God's earth did you find it, man?' he breathed.

In answer, Professor Challoner leaned back in his chair, reached out one spindly arm, and passed his leathern hand vaguely over the antique globe that stood beside him.

'We left for the Congo,' he began, 'on the 14th November last, from Marble Arch.'

'The Greenline eh?' muttered Frobisher admiringly. 'You were taking a bit of a chance. Dorking can be a bugger in the rainy season.'

Challoner smiled.

'Not,' he said, 'if you know your way around. By nightfall, we were in East Sweden.'

Twistleton-Wickham-Finkel, who had been jotting frantically upon a piece of Club notepaper, glanced up at me.

'He must have gone over the Brenner,' he said, 'and

dropped down into Cork. From there, it's no more than an hour's run to Lagos, if the tide's with you.'

'Just so,' said Challoner. 'We made camp in a little clearing just outside Vitry-sur-Marne. . .'

'I know it well!' cried Frobisher excitedly. 'There's what they call a *Little Chef* on the corner where they roll the meat into sort of tiny flat patties and stick them into a kind of round cake. I have a photograph somewhere that one of my bearers took of me holding a giant rubber tomato. It was during my last abortive attempt on the Eiger, when they took off the restaurant car at, was it Melbourne, and we all had to hitchhike back through the Camargue.'

'. . .and,' continued Challoner, fixing Frobisher with a terrible glance, 'upon the following morning, we set out across the veldt towards Cowes.'

'Shark country,' grunted Twistleton-Wickham-Finkel. 'You were damned lucky, Challoner!'

'Not luck, I fancy,' said I. 'Challoner is an old Arctic hand. You forget, Twinkers, that Challoner was the first chap to stumble on the North-West Passage, weren't you, old man?'

Challoner sighed deeply. Time glazed his cornflower eyes.

'They were asking £39,250 for it,' he said. 'It was a lot of money in those days. Plus it needed a fortune spent on it. It had an outside khazi, you know.'

'What happened?' enquired Frobisher, pushing King Solomon's Chicken aside to discourage the bluebottles.

'I offered thirty, but the Norwegians beat me to it.'

'Bad show!'

'At least,' said Challoner, 'I assume they were Norwegians. Big black buggers in a clapped-out 1953 Consul.'

'Anyway,' I said, for I sensed the old melancholy was about to settle on our great narrator, 'you got to Cowes without any difficulty?'

'More or less, more or less,' replied Challoner. 'We had something of a communications problem at the Italian frontier, mind. They had a sign up saying *Private Estate* in English, and I thought to myself, aha, this is doubtless the aftermath of the Asian Cup Final, they are trying to keep the Brits out, well, Johnny Wop, I thought, you have to get up bloody early in the morning to catch old Mister Challoner! There was this dago sitting by the barrier in some kind of pansy uniform, so I reckoned if I threw a string of onions round my neck and addressed him in his own language—in which I happen, of course, to be fluent—he would take me to be a local and wave me through.'

'Did it work?' asked Frobisher.

'Did it hell,' said Challoner. 'I marched up to him and I said *Guten Morgen, ich bin auf dem weg nach Cowes,* and the next thing I knew this damned great dog of his was chasing us all down the road towards Leningrad. I never saw my porters again.'

'Probably all holed up in Leningrad,' muttered Twistleton-Wickham-Finkel, 'with a dozen belly-dancers and a crate of Guinness. What did you do?'

'Fortunately,' replied Challoner, 'they'd left me the map. It was the work of a moment to pinpoint Tchad, take a couple of quick bearings, and set off North up the A40.'

'Keeping a weather-eye open for the Khmer Rouge?' put in Frobisher.

'Keeping a weather-eye open for Khmer Rouge, yes,' said Challoner.

'For God's sake stop interrupting!' snapped Twistleton-Wickham-Finkel, 'or we'll never get to King Solomon's Chicken. By the way, why are its giblets in a little bag?'

'Ah,' said Challoner, 'I was coming to that.'

As well he might have, had, at that moment, the most fearful commotion not broken out in the hallway beyond the library. There were roars, there were cries, there were cheers, there were huzzahs and shrieks and whistles and snatches of song and the sound of dinner gongs being peremptorily struck!

Alas for poor Challoner and his tale, I am sorry to say we all sprang from our chairs and rushed to investigate the source of the uproar. Nor did we have far to rush, since hardly had we left our alcove than the doors of the library were flung apart to admit an ecstatic mob bearing upon their shoulders a figure at whose sight we could but reel and gasp!

'It cannot be!' I cried.

'It is quite impossible!' shouted Frobisher.

'Is it really you?' shrieked Twistleton-Wickham-Finkel.

At this last hysterical address the elegant figure smiled, and looked down benignly upon us.

'Yes,' said Phileas Fogg, 'it is really I!'

'But,' cried Frobisher, waving his turnip watch, 'it is only the first of July! You have succeeded in circumnavigating the globe not in eighty days, but in a mere forty-five! How can this be?'

Lithely, the great traveller dropped from the acclamatory shoulders and shook our out-stretched hands.

'As good fortune would have it,' said Fogg, 'the completion of the M25 enabled me to by-pass China completely.'

Professor Challoner carefully prodded the giblets back inside King Solomon's Chicken and replaced it in its cardboard box.

'Hardly sporting,' he muttered. 'In my day, we had to swim China.'

Time On My Hand

LURCH AWAKE, in impenetrable dark.

Half awake.

Tiny, far-off, metallic, rhythmic tink-tink-bing-bing-bing, tink-tink-bing-bing, like weeny hammer striking weeny nail, ringingly. What going on? Elves at work behind skirting, preparations for Mouse Queen wedding, get bloody move on, Nitkin, pull finger out, Titkin, golden coach two days behind schedule as per yours of 15th ultimo, where rear-end differential, where tiara rack, Mouse Queen go mad, Mouse King eat night shift, never mind *Hi-ho, hi-ho*, get bloody skates on?

Three-quarters awake.

Noise not elves, noise coming from bedside table, elves never work on bedside table, could get flattened by outflung hand seeking, e.g., new Jap watch, six months work on gold coach down drain, little wheels fly everywhere, little windows shattered, little Titkin knocked senseless into ashtray, little Nitkin hurled into unfinished Remy Martin nightcap, unable to climb out of balloon glass, blind drunk in ten minutes, Mouse Queen go mad, Mouse King bite heads off.

Elf scenario fades. Fully awake, now. Noise coming from new Jap watch; it NJW alarm, it time to get up, say NJW, it time to put ten yen in parking meter, it time for meeting with Chairman Nakimoto San, it time for origami class, it time to chuck unworthy self on sword.

What time, exactly?

NJW not luminous, cannot find NJW in dark, let alone time it got, NJW got four buttons controlling eight million different functions including little light, grope for watch, knock over nightcap, find wet NJW, luckily waterproof to two hundred metres according to huge owner's manual, no mention of brandyproof depth, mind, could be conked out by now, take it back, man in Dixon's Holborn Circus take one look, bow, say So sorry, customer-san, you infringe guarantee, how about you buy brandyproof model, only £18.99, it good for two hundred metres, also got breathalyser function, also go tink-tink-bing-bing ten minutes before drink-up time so customer-san get two more rounds in?

Wife beginning to stir, tink-tink-bing-bing beginning to penetrate, grab wet NJW, hobble into bathroom to put on light to see watch in order to locate right button to put on watch-light to see watch. . .

It 3.40 am

Why alarm go off at 3.40 am? It not programmed by me, cannot programme alarm at all, bought watch this morning, took me three hours to set ordinary time, watch got umpteen modes and four buttons, i.e. umpteen^4 = possibility of hitting right formula for setting time, watch kept going into peculiar spasm, lap-times, stop-watching, countdowns, kept nearly getting time-setting mode, get date right, dial TIM, wait for bleep, press button, entire display vanish again, watch play *Bluebells of Scotland,* try again, this time watch play *Humoresque,* NJW got five different alarm tunes *plus* tink-tink-bing-bing, it like having radiogram on wrist, spent entire morning listening to tinny medley of old tat, finally, more luck than judgement, got watch to tell time. Never touched alarm mode.

3.42. Still going tink-tink-bing-bing, must be way of stopping it, dare not push knob at random, might lose time display again, might get *O Mine Papa,* wife wake up, wife claim man sitting on bidet at 3.43 playing *O Mine Papa* on watch incontrovertible grounds for quickie divorce, wife snatch up children, vanish, leave customer-san staring at car vanishing up road with watch playing *Hello dolly!* to rest of street, lights go on, windows open, neighbours get restraining order, customer-san end up in Broadmoor with NJW playing *God Save the King* endlessly, cannot stop watch by banging it on padded wall, watch guaranteed shockproof, would have to dive into something over two hundred metres deep to stop it, they not have two-hundred-metres-deep things in Broadmoor, Broadmoor not allow inmate-san to hurt self, Broadmoor got rubber spoons, Broadmoor got wooden scissors.

3.45. Watch suddenly stop of own accord.

Stare at watch.

Did not want all this.

Had nice old gold Omega, went on holiday last week, NOGO not good to two hundred metres, NOGO turn out not even good to one metre, come out of pool, NOGO no go. Came home, took it to NOGO agent, NOGO agent say waterproofing up spout, watch now full of teeny dried plankton etc. like whale's lower set, fifty quid to recondition.

Think. Not worth it, could buy brand new watch for half that, seen them in Dixon's Holborn Circus, stick NOGO in pocket, walk to Dixon's, Dixon's got huge display of winking dials, showcase look like 747 dashboard, how to choose? This one got nine million functions, including calculator mode and international bus time-table, that one patched into Pentagon database and Dow Jones update, one over there got David and Igor Oistrakh playing Bach Double Violin Concerto every hour, tell assistant-san want watch that just tell time, assistant-san chuckle, for only £17.99 customer-san get entire bag of tricks, this 1984, customer-san, what for you want £7.99 banger, for extra tenner customer-san walk tall, do own Olympic sprint timing to fourteen decimal places, settle argument in Athenaeum over tallest building in Latvia, dive down to inspect *Mary Rose* while playing full hour of Val Doonican's Greatest Hits.

Give assistant-san £17.99, drive home, something in glove compartment playing *O Mine Papa*, get home, study manual, e.g:

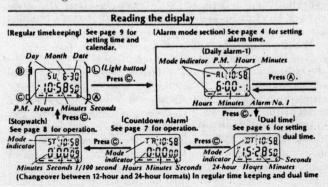

Reading the display

[Regular timekeeping] See page 9 for setting time and calendar.

[Alarm mode section] See page 4 for setting alarm time.

Day Month Date

(Light button) Press ©.

P.M. Hours Minutes Seconds Press ©.

(Daily alarm-1) Mode indicator P.M. Hours Minutes

Hours Minutes Alarm No. 1

Press ©.

[Stopwatch] See page 8 for operation. Mode indicator Press ©. [Countdown Alarm] See page 7 for operation. Mode indicator Press ©. [Dual time] See page 6 for setting dual time. Mode indicator Seconds

Minutes Seconds 1/100 second Hours Minutes Seconds 24-hour Hours Minutes

(Changeover between 12-hour and 24-hour formats) In regular time keeping and dual time

After entire morning, completely stumped.

It tragic story of age, it some kind of Parkinson Law, man constantly buying more and more things with unusable extras just because unusable extras come cheap, man buy wallet, wallet got ballpoint in it, man already got ballpoint, now not only got unnecessary ballpoint, unnecessary ballpoint got tiny calculator on it at no extra charge, unnecessary tiny calculator got trigonometry mode, man now spend all day working out height of trees.

Never mind computers. Half homes in country now got little tin box bought to do milk bills plus occasional hand of whist, but discovered to be capable of umpteen totally unnecessary functions, customers must amortize £299.95, therefore half homes in country up most of night writing unnecessary programmes, other half up most of night wondering whether to give in and buy one, entire country fall into bed, knackered, at 2 am, NJW go off at 3.40, everybody wake up again.

Something behind all this. Plot.

Stare at watch again

Why NJW go off at 3.40?

NJW obviously programmed in factory to go off at 3.40, must be 6.40 in Tokyo, all watches go off, everybody-san get up, chop-chop, everybody scuttle down Datsubishi factory, shipyard, NJW watchworks, everybody start toiling away nineteen to dozen, make ten million exports before *Bluebells of Scotland* inform them it time for 2.34 minute lunchbreak, set lapsed-time mode to 2.34 minutes, gobble sukiyaki, watch play *Hello Dolly (Herro Dorry?)*, everybody rush back to workbench, graft graft, graft, export watches to Britain, Brits go into Dixon's Holborn Circus, buy NJW.

Wake up at 3.40 in morning.

Not fit for work next day, make half a Metro, put two rivets in three-year-overdue oil-rig, fall off quarter-built skyscraper, British economy go down tubes, Nippon triumphant, Queen step down, Hirohito troop colour.

4.12 am.

Look out of bathroom window.

Rising sun in east.

Anything Legal Considered

Next week 21,000 members of the American Bar Association descend on London for their annual conference.

Guardian

MS LOIS SHOEMAKER
Bidwell,Kreis & Runningwolf
234 E 56th Street NYC

July 5

Dear Ms Shoemaker,

Oh wow, did we have a terrific flight! We had the best flight we ever had! We had one of those flights you want to hang on to for when the bad days come around and you need something to, you know, remind you of the way it was, once.

Remember you pre-booked us two forward aisle seats, non-smoking? Know what the dummies did? The dummies stuck us aft, window-seats, smoking, that's what the dummies did! The creep on my left was chain-smoking black stogies, the broad in front was dropping Marlboro stubs all over, not only did Mrs Bidwell get maybe the worst attack of asthma since we took sixteen grand off of General Motors for the air-conditioning hitting the fritz in the Lincoln Tunnel but I got lucky, too, the broad burned a hole in my new Gucci iguana-hide zipper-bag! And you want to know better yet? Better yet is I bend down to put the bagfire out and when I straighten up – you're never going to believe this – I gash my head on the tray which has accidentally opened, there was blood all over, including my new Bugatti silk tie which is an original model!

Please look out the Ginsberg vs. TWA file and forward Xerox urgentest. I figure twenty-five grand for the asthma, minimum, plus another twenty for distress at iguana wipe-out, plus we could definitely be looking at fifty G's for the gash, it goes way across the forehead, with any luck I will have a major scar, I could've lost a whole eye, but who can have everything, be content, don't be greedy, don't I tell clients that all the time, if God had wanted me to lose an eye He would've made bigger trays, is how I look at it.

Fortunately, there was a doctor on board who rushed over and put a couple of stitches in the cut. Am I a lucky guy, or am I a lucky guy? Have you any idea of the kind of malpractice suit we're talking here, Ms Shoemaker, I been in this business a long time, nobody is gonna tell me this quack's training involved sinking four vodkatinis and sewing a head at 40,000 feet, I could walk out of that court-room a yacht owner, Ms Shoemaker, I could be looking at a chateau.

The only downer is where Schwartzbart of Schwartzbart, Schwartzbart, Dreck and Schwarzbart beat me to a cab at Heathrow by jumping the queue. I could've had him on maybe three different counts, but Jack Schwartzbart is one smart shyster, you would not believe the counter-claims he could pull, Dreck I could make mincemeat of but I am not going up against Jack Schwartzbart, it would be goodbye chateau.

Please forward Kowalski vs. The Denver Water Authority. I think I tasted fluoride in my toothmug this morning.

Sincerely,
Samuel D. Bidwell

MS LOIS SHOEMAKER
Bidwell, Kreis & Runningwolf
234 E 56th Street NYC

July 7

Dear Ms Shoemaker,
Jesus, this is a terrific town! Just walking around it, you keep saying to yourself *This town is anything up to a hundred years old!* The sidewalks are all shot, the doorways are all kind of low and saggy, the walls are damp, the floorboards creak, so far we have twisted two ankles, wiped out an entire hat, caught two real big viral infections, and been up the whole damn night! I hate to be a pain, but could you forward Henshawe vs. Poughkeepsie Tarmacadam Inc., Pinchus vs. The Groton Old Innes Corp., McKinnoch vs. Tombstone Health & Welfare, and Dinkheim vs. Achison, Topeka and Santa Fe?

Mrs Bidwell says if this all works out right, we could maybe go to a full-mouth reconstruction in 22-carat, plus throw in a couple of new boobs. I sure hope so, I love that woman, Ms Shoemaker, I would not like her to get second-bested by Mrs Harry Stonewort. Remember Stonewort, Klein, Klein & Rimmell? They all went off to some toney restaurant, they hit a wrong crab, both Kleins had to get pumped out and Harry Stonewort may have permanent liver damage, this is a million-dollar touch, Ms Shoemaker, this is Charlie Q. Big One, this is where the Stoneworts get the ten-thousand-acre ranch with the reproduction hacienda plus mineral rights! I could've joined them at that goddam restaurant, Ms Shoemaker, they asked me, they wanted to discuss the tall Klein's case against being stuck in the room reserved for the small Klein, but what did I do, I had room service on account of this virus I picked up at St Paul's Column. All I got off room service was a fishbone in the throat, five thousand bucks, tops, due to where they are bound to go for contributory negligence.

Still, Rimmell's the guy I'm really sorry for. He don't eat crab, so he ordered the melon on account of melon always gives him diarrhoea, and you know what? *Nothing!* Not even a lousy hundred-dollar flatulence suit. I guess they have different melons in Europe, it is something they ought to tell you about in law school, I wonder if Rimmell has a case against Harvard, it is worth looking into.

Please add Perry vs. Ogenbogen Glass & Sundries. It is not fluoride, it is definitely something in the goddam beaker, you can smell it even when it is empty.

Sincerely,
Samuel D. Bidwell

MS LOIS SHOEMAKER
Bidwell, Kreis & Runningwolf
234 E 56th Street NYC

July 8

Dear Ms Shoemaker,

Is mortification the word? I am not too big on fancy stuff, you have seen me in court, you know me, Ms Shoemaker, Honest Sam Bidwell, call a spade a spade, I stand in the proud heritage of Abe Lincoln, what the hell use is a long word when a short one will do, they ain't paying you by the syllable, is my view.

You will not believe this, Ms Shoemaker. I advise you to sit down before reading further. I do not want you to fall off your chair and bring some damn fool action for negligence or actual physical distress or misuse of the mails or sexual belligerence or I don't know what else.

The fact is, I am being sued by Charlie Runningwolf. Not only am I being sued by a junior partner, I am being sued by a *red* junior partner, I am being sued by a Pawnee junior partner, it will teach us to be an equal opportunities employer, Ms Shoemaker, it will teach us to bring these dingbats off the reservation and show them how to tie shoes, please shred this letter, I do not wish to be looking at the wrong end of Giant Moose Who Stands By The Still Water vs. Friendly Trucking Inc.

Last night, while Mrs Bidwell and I were swallowing our chest medication prior to strolling abroad in the hope of running across some mugger prepared to allow us to take the British Government for all it has – you would not believe the very sweet Criminal Compensation loopholes they have here, Ms Shoemaker – our telephone rang.

It was Charlie Runningwolf, in Room 213. 'I am in Room 213,' he said, 'and I am staring at the goddam garage. How come you look out over the frigging park and all I have is the frigging gas pumps?'

I explained to him that it was on account of he was a junior partner, but he became extremely abusive, implying strongly that

31

it was in fact on account of he was red. He pointed out that his people had been systematically dispossessed, raped, pillaged, butchered and incinerated, and on top of all this, they were now being asked to stay in a room with a view of the Texaco forecourt!

He sounded canned to me, Ms Shoemaker, so I told him to lay off the firewater. The next thing I know, that little wall-eyed dyke Phoebe Lumachi from Lumachi, Gimmer, Birnbaum, Twisk & Donghoffer is at my door with a writ.

'Not only are we as of this moment in time Lumachi, Gimmer, Birnbaum, Twisk, Donghoffer & Runningwolf,' she smirks, 'but we also represent Mr Charles Runningwolf in the little matter of Runningwolf vs. Bidwell. Boy-oh-boy, fartface, is that firewater crack gonna *cost!*'

The upshot, Ms Shoemaker, is I am being hit on eight different discrimination counts, plus professional misconduct, plus a whole new juridical gizmo thought up by this Lumachi dame, to wit, and I quote, 'Misleading a desk clerk as to the personal habits of an Original American in order to gain favourable treatment.'

I intend fighting this one all the way up to the Supreme Court, starting with Room 213.

Sincerely,
Samuel D. Bidwell

MS LOIS SHOEMAKER
Kreis
234 E 56th Street NYC

July 9

Dear Lois,

I feel I can call you Lois, I hope you don't mind, the last thing I want is a major condescension suit just when things are going so well, also not using your surname is probably an infringement of your civil liberties etcetera, I do not know about these things, my dear husband never kept me, you know, abreast of the law, maybe he figured I'd run out on him if I got to understand the paperwork involved.

Anyway.

Last night, right after he mailed your letter, he rushed up to see Charlie Runningwolf in 213, I was real worried, he did not take the lift, his blood pressure is already 190 over 130, if he dropped dead in the lift we could take Otis to the cleaners, but if he dropped dead on the stairs, that one is down to him, zilch for the estate, unless you can prove a loose stair-rod, never easy, we tried that time in, was it Heidelberg, anyway, he was carrying maybe two hundred pages of notes, he was fixing to get that red gonnof on everything from inside trading and telephone assault to conduct abroad likely to bring the United States of, you know, America into disrepute, plus he reckoned to subpoena Lumachi, Gimmer, Birnbaum, Twisk and Donghoffer as material witnesses on sixty-seven counts. i.e. keep the bastards in court until around 1998, no work coming in, fix their wagon real permanent, all that, so he bangs on the door, and he stomps in, and he begins handing out the writs, and Charlie Runningwolf sinks a tomahawk in his head.

I just noticed a typing error, Ms Shoemaker, paragraph one, I am not too good with these British manual machines, that should read my *dead* husband, sorry.

Anyway, what I want to know is, how much is Charlie Runningwolf good for on his personal account? I am out one top breadwinner, plus grief-stricken to the tune of, who knows, with a smart lawyer could be as much as five million. Thinking of which, forget that little wimp Kreis, I was thinking of retaining this Phoebe Lumachi, she is one sharp cookie, could *she* represent me in Bidwell vs. Runningwolf, even though the red dummy is her junior partner?

Or would that be—what's the word—unethical?

Yours truly,
Miriam Bidwell

Cry Havoc!

An EEC plan to tattoo dogs and cats with identification marks has brought howls of protest from British MEPs.

Daily Star

'IN THE nightmare of the dark,' murmured the Irish setter, 'all the dogs of Europe bark.'

The others stopped rooting in their matted groins, and glanced up.

'Auden,' explained the Irish setter.

'Clever sod.' said the sealyham.

'On the death of Yeats,'said the setter, softly.

'Dead is he, Yeats?' enquired the alsatian.

Moisture gleamed in the setter's limpid eye.

'Begob, yes,' he said.

The alsation cleared its dreadful throat.

'This Auden,' he murmured, 'I don't suppose he said where the bones were buried?'

There was- an inevitable, though fortunately brief, skirmish, during which, with equal inevitability, the setter lost most of one ear. It retired bitterly behind a gravel bin, where it could subsequently be heard crooning, low, an ancient John McCormack ballad.

'You realise,' said the bulldog, 'that if he'd had his EEC tattoo on that ear, he'd be bloody anonymous by now?'

'It only goes to show,' said the alsatian. 'They live in another world, committees. It is easy to tell no-one up Strasbourg has ever been a dog.'

'Funny really,' said a collie, with all the thoughtfulness of his breed, 'them being Alsatians and so forth.'

'Good point,' said the alsatian, nodding. 'Except I am strictly speaking a German shepherd.'

'You don't want to nod,' said the sealyham, albeit respectfully. 'You look like something in the back of a Cortina.'

The alsatian ignored this.

'As a German shepherd,' it said, 'I should expect to be tattooed under my left foreleg. It was common practice up the SS, and I do not see any reason to change a winning formula.'

'As a *genuine* German,' put in a hitherto silent dachshund, heavily, 'as a *genuine* German who had no idea what was going on, I should object most strongly to being tattooed under my left foreleg.'

'You and the tattooist both,' said the alsatian, with a fanged snigger. 'He'd have to be a midget to start with, never mind getting on his back and sliding underneath, why don't you ask him to drain the sump and look at the front suspension while he's down there?'

The other dogs laughed to see such fun; or, more accurately, to avoid going summarily monaural.

'Be that as it may,' said the bulldog, 'it is nevertheless concealing a serious point, i.e. where will it end? Start with tattooed ears, next thing you know it will be widdling on the right. Don't talk to me about bureaucracy, I nearly got put down once for doing a gasman's shin, if it hadn't been for the *Sunday Express* and eight million *News At Ten* supporters, I should very likely be two dozen spring rolls by now.'

'Standardisation is the enemy,' said the sealyham.

They looked at it.

'He don't half come out with 'em,' said the bulldog, 'for something that looks like a sink tidy.'

The setter let out a low ululating approximation to *Danny Boy.*

'I was very much against letting the Irish enter in the first place,' said the alsatian. 'I knew we'd get this, singing, violence, sod-all constructive. I think they all ought to have special tattoos. Big yellow shamrocks, something of that order.'

The others pondered this uneasily.

'It doesn't sound very European,' murmured the collie, finally. 'It does not seem to be in, er, line with current ecumenical thinking.'

'Good,' said the alsatian. 'I know about these things, before you look round there'll be a bloody Irish setter mountain.'

'If God had wanted us standardised,' continued the sealyham more or less to itself, 'He would have made us cats.'

'I'd gas cats,' said the alsatian.

'My personal view about tattoos,' said the bulldog, 'is they should have a ship that sinks when you breathe in.'

'Funny that, coming from you,' said the dachshund.

'I think there may be a personal remark coming up,' said a poodle.

'Watch it,' said the bulldog, between pants.

'No offence meant' said the dachshund, 'we must all breathe in our own individual ways—'

'God,' growled the alsatian, 'I hate the new Germany!'

'—I just meant it would look a trifle unbecoming. Not ever sinking, just bobbing up and down two hundred times a minute. I'm not saying it's your fault, or anything.'

'Here,' said the alsatian to the bulldog, 'you're not deformed, I trust? We don't want nothing deformed in Europe, if you're deformed we might as well string you up now instead of buggering about with tattoos etcetera, all that paperwork.'

'Try it,' muttered the bulldog.

'I think we're getting away from the main issue,' said the poodle.

'A decadent speaks,' said the alsatian.

The poodle tossed its head.

'The main issue, as I see it,' it went on, 'concerns what might best be described as the Eurodog Concept.'

'Hallo,' said the bulldog, wrinkling an already striated forehead until it resembled an estuary foreshore.

'Intellectuals,' muttered the alsatian, rolling its terrible eyes so that they took on the ochreous semblance of unborn eggs. 'Hard labour is the only answer.'

'In other words,' persisted the poodle, 'do we feel tattooing will unify us into common Eurocaninity, or alternatively, rob us of our individual sovereign identities?'

The alsatian stared at it for a time; then, slowly, turned its head towards the other dogs.

'What *is* it about the French?' it said.

'Speaking for myself,' said the dachshund, carefully, 'and recognising that the past is now behind us, i.e. one hundred per cent of dachshunds now living were born after 1945, I nevertheless feel that Eurocaninity could easily lead to mongrelism, which I personally would deplore.'

'Not hard to see why,' said the alsatian, smirking. 'Given a Common Genocultural Policy and your average bureaucratic, if you'll pardon the expression, cock-up, you could well find yourself sharing a Eurobreeding kennel with e.g., a Great Dane or similar. Not,' it added smartly, 'that I do not go along with your views on racial purity, indeed it bucks me up no end, it is quite clear that the dachshund doesn't fall far from the tree, as it were. We shall be,' and here it turned slyly to the poodle, 'back across the Rhine in two shakes of a, of a–'

The silence that followed was fraught, brief, and broken by the bulldog's easing itself slowly off its tiny haunches the better to shove forward its heavily muscled shoulders, and say, breathily:

'That was well out of order.'

'Oh really?' said the alsatian, and sank its teeth into the poodle's neck.

Whereupon the bulldog lurched with surprising agility, and clamped its fearful jaws over the alsatian's thigh, which left the dachshund with little alternative but to lock on to the bulldog's ear, despite the inevitable consequences to itself of having its tail immediately pincered by the collie, whose views on devolution were as tenuous as the Home Rule stance of a Welsh corgi now frantically attempting to snap at what historians would doubtless refer to, albeit euphemistically, as the soft underbelly of the alsatian.

Only the Irish setter, aloof from the Eurocidal melee beyond its gravel-bin, remained—of course—neutral.

'And the living nations wait,' it recited, 'Each sequestered in its hate.'

It looked around for someone to appreciate this, and found only a fat Russian Blue, who had been observing the proceedings from the secure position of its tree, high above.

'Auden,' explained the setter.

The Russian Blue merely blinked impassively. Not only did it not speak dog, it did not give a damn either way. It knew only that, all things considered, it could not be long before the cats inherited the earth.

Man-Eating Batsmen of Death-Ray Island

A Full Length Yuletide Yarn

'NATIVE WAR canoes coming this way?' cried Flight Sergeant 'Footy' Boote VC, two-fisted ginger-mopped Headmaster of The School That Would Not Die. 'Are you sure?'

In answer, Beaky Finkel, madcap tailor of the Remove, whipped out the hundred-inch refracting telescope he had made just that morning from two old cocoa-tins and a broken ping-pong bat, and put it to his eye.

'Yes, skipper, it's a dusky band all right,' he retorted, shinning rapidly down the yucca tree again, 'and what's more, they've got Johnny Dodds on clarinet! Of course, it might just be a devilish Hun trick!'

His plucky Headmaster considered this for a moment, cocking an ear for the insistent beat of distant drums echoing across The Lagoon They Could Not Smell.

'*King Porter Stomp,*' he mused aloud. 'Do you know, Beaky, I think you may be spot on. I happen to know that Obersturmbanngruppenführer Herman 'Spotty' Knackwurst, The Nazi That Time Forgot, went missing not twenty miles from here while trying to snare The Giant Squid Of Atlantis, which his fiendish bosses back in Berlin planned to clone in the laboratories of kindly old Professor Mondieu, whose lovely young daughter was being held to ransom by The Panzers Of The Damned. Tall and blonde, too, I hasten to add.'

'Hum! Sho' sound like dat ole Nazi up to his tricks again! Only one name fo' a man messin' aroun' wid a tall blonde squid!'

The speaker was none other than Prince Nbing Nbong, known as Shine to his chums in the Remedial Shell, who had hurtled faithfully up on his trusty monocycle at the first inkling of trouble, and was now wrinkling his dusky brow, as was his native wont. How they all chuckled! Footy Boote clapped him on the back so smartly that the multimillionaire paramount chief's enormous eyes rolled around in his gleaming ebony head like marbles in a saucer!

'God bless my soul, Shine,' he cried, 'what a jolly old black scallywag you are! It was the *daughter* who was tall and blonde, ha-ha-ha!'

'Ha-ha-ha!' shrieked The School That Would Not Die dutifully, rolling around among the coconuts, and trying to imagine how jolly rotten it must be to be a tall blonde daughter with your skirt ripped to the thigh and buttons bursting off your blouse while beastly Boche tank commanders tried to get you to play doctors and nurses with them.

'The Giant Squid, on the other hand,' continued Footy Boote, drawing reflectively on The Trusty Briar From Outer Space, 'was an extremely unsavoury cove—Johnny Hun planned to make a thousand of them, you know, and parachute them all over the Home Counties, prior to the invasion. Can you imagine what havoc they would have wrought, and not just on the County Cricket Championship?' His bright carrot-red hair grew serious for a moment. 'Can any of us say for sure how he would have reacted if he had found a Giant Squid doing things to his sister?'

'I should have run the pair of them through!' cried Corky Lino, The Centre Half With The Dynamite Studs.

'Well said, Corky!' bellowed his trusty Head. 'Best be on the safe side, eh?'

The chaps all nodded. Sage old Footy Boote VC! He had his head screwed on all right, for a beak. It was common sense like his that had seen them through all the hair-raising escapades that had befallen them ever since the ship taking them to New Zealand for their annual rugger fixture had been torpedoed by the devilish Japs and they had been luckily plucked out of the ocean by albatrosses and deposited here on The Island From One Million BC, miles from the trade routes, where dinosaurs, because of a unique medicinal fern, still roamed, laying the eggs with which The School That Would Not Die was able to supplement the diet of roots and berries they had been able to identify from *Ye Booke of South Sea Rootes and Berrys* that Buggy Bolsover had found mysteriously wrapped in a yellow oilskin pouch inside the hollow tree he had been using to practice ventriloquism in case cannibals turned up and needed to be scared off by talking shrubs.

It was Buggy who stood up now, as the drums throbbed ever closer.

'Do you think I should get inside the tree, skipper?' he enquired. 'We ought to be ready when the war canoes hit the beach!'

In answer, Footy slapped him on the shoulder with such force that Buggy's startled exclamation appeared to come from a boulder two hundred yards away, fortunately thwarting a column of giant ants who had, unbeknownst to the chaps, been bearing down on them with a view to stripping their bones bare in seconds!

'Lord bless you, no, Buggy!' cried the cheery Head. 'I have no intention of letting our chum Johnny Man-Eater ever reach the beach! I intend borrowing Desmond d'Arcy's monocle and focussing the sun's rays on the canoes so that the tinder-dry animal skins catch fire and sink, precipitating our dusky adversaries into the shark-infested waters!'

'But isn't that just what they'll be expecting, sir?' enquired Lawrence 'Tiny' Featherstonehaugh, The Fat Boy With Surprising Agility For One So Large.

'That's a chance we'll just have to take!' riposted Flight Sergeant Boote, raising his aquiline nose and sniffing expertly. 'Fortunately, the wind has just changed in our favour!'

The chaps all nodded. Sage old Footy Boote VC! He had his head screwed on all right, for a beak.

Desmond d'Arcy, however, took leave to demur.

'It'll take more than my old monocle, sir,' opined that worthy. 'Those canoes must be two miles off. I rather doubt that we can focus the sun's rays effectively over that distance.'

Beaky Finkel, madcap tailor of the Remove, who had been sketching some rapid equations in the dust with a sharp stick, now looked up.

'It's perfectly possible, chaps,' he said, quietly. 'It's all a question of physics.'

The School That Would Not Die gazed at him in admiration.

'Go on Beaky,' muttered Footy, through clenched teeth.

'Basically,' explained the wily Levantine, 'I shall need sixty-three cocoa-tins.'

'Then there's no time to be lost!' roared the Head. 'Scour the island, you chaps!'

As one man, the plucky lads leapt up and plunged into the scrub, heedless of the poisonous giant thorns stabbing at their sinewy limbs, which – thanks to an antidote made from giant jellyfish that 'Stinks' Cholmondeley-Cholmondeley, The Masked Chemist Who Rode With The Quorn, had accidentally stumbled upon while diving for The Lost Hoard Of Captain Blood – were now not only immune to the deadly barbs, but incredibly strengthened, enabling all of them to run the hundred yards in under five seconds, a skill which, regular readers will recall, had stood them in particularly good stead The Night The Saucer Landed.

Nevertheless, a good ten minutes had passed before they reassembled, dropping their gathered cocoa-tins at the feet of Beaky Finkel.

'Well done!' cried Footy Boote VC. 'I'd been rather dreading the news that they had all been trampled by dinosaurs. He's a delicate thing, your Johnny Cocoa-Tin!'

'Right first time, skipper!' retorted Corky Lino. '*We did* find that a number *had* been flattened, but, as luck would have it, Shine here stumbled into an old disused elephant trap, and what do you suppose was at the bottom of it?'

'Shine, at a guess!' cried Footy Boote, quick as a flash.

How they all chortled, not least the big darkie, despite the two broken legs, which, in a white man, might have been very serious, but which, because of the many years of dancing, were in Prince Nbing Nbong's case so strongly reinforced by muscle that he felt no more pain than if he had fallen on his massively boned head.

'Yassum, baas, dat sho' true, ah *was* at de bottom ob de hole,' laughed the latter, 'but dat weren't de only ting down dere. What ah foun' wuz de remains of a Fust Worl' War zeppelin, shot down by curare-tipped pyggermy arrows while ferryin' a cargo o' tinned cocoa to a German climbin' team trapped by lava unexpectedly whizzin f'om de mouf o' De Volcano Dat Nobody Noo!'

'Good work, Shine!' cried Footy Boote VC.

'Now, off you go, and wrap some incredibly restorative

gully-gully leaves around those legs of yours, you'll be going in third wicket down after we've seen your coon cousins off, and if there's no fancy work off the front foot, I shall be down on you like the proverbial ton of bricks!'

Thus congratulated by the fellow he loved most in all the world, the sheepishly grinning giant loped happily away, while the rest of the chaps gathered around Beaky Finkel, whose dextrous ring-spanners, cunningly fashioned from a triceratops rib-cage, were already flashing among the cocoa-tins, faster than the eye could follow!

Five minutes and some pretty swift hammering later, the madcap tailor's masterpiece stood revealed. A great gasp went up from the assembled chums!

'I say, Beaky, old sport,' cried Corky Lino, voicing everyone's unspoken thoughts, 'what on earth *is* that extraordinary contraption?'

It was Beaky's turn to chuckle.

'It may be just an extraordinary contraption to you,' he said, 'but to me it's sixty-three cocoa-tins with d'Arcy's monocle wedged in the end.'

Footy Boote pursed his lips and let out a low whistle.

'I call it,' said Beaky, 'my Death Ray!'

In the ensuing silence, you could have heard the proverbial pin drop!

'Wow!' called Prince Nbing Nbong, from his little compound, 'Man hab bin lookin' fo' de secret ob de Def Ray since de beginnin' ob time.'

'But it took Beaky here to find it!' exclaimed the Head. 'What a dashed clever race they are, albeit a trifle short in the slow left-arm spin department. What say we take it down to the beach, chaps, and give our visitors the shock of their jolly old lives?'

The boys needed no second bidding. With great whoops, they sped through the scrub on sturdy limbs, bearing the precious death ray on their tanned shoulders, and did not stop until their pounding feet met the bone-white sand.

Where they suddenly fetched up, their eyes on stalks, their mouths agape!

'Curses!' cried Footy Boote. 'There's one thing we reckoned without!'

'You mean—?' muttered an anguished Corky.

'Exactly!' retorted the plucky Head, smiting himse.. the brow and silently cursing himself for a fool. 'The Tia.. Wave That Came From Nowhere!'

For, while they had been busy at their various tasks, they had not realised quite how rapidly the native canoes had sped shorewards! Even now, the howling Hottentots were hurtling up the beach towards them, shrunken skulls rattling at their skimpily clad waists, their sinewy hands brandishing the murderous cricket bats retrieved from the wreck of HMS Spofforth after that fine ship had struck a Japanese mine while bound for Guadalcanal with The Team That Would Go Anywhere For a Game!

'I'm afraid my death ray is no use at this range, skipper!' cried Beaky Finkel.

'And even if it were,' muttered Footy Boote, knotting his muscles and preparing to sell himself dearly with several clean uppercuts of his own design, 'I fear it would be no match for honest British willow!'

Whereupon, setting jaws and gritting teeth, The School That Would Not Die formed, as their plucky ancestors had done, a square, and got ready to go down fighting!

And then, suddenly, without any warning, the sky became absolutely pitch-black! As one animal, the gleaming savages came to a confused stop, muttering and mumbling, until all that the brave lads could see in the inky gloom was eyeballs and teeth!

'What the—?' snapped Corky Lino.

'Just hold on!' hissed Flight Sergeant Footy Boote VC. 'For, unless I am very much mistaken—'

He was not. A split-second later, the queer tropical darkness was suddenly lit by eerie flashes of light that hissed and crackled in the very air above the beach, to be followed by what seemed to be glowing footballs bouncing astonishingly from tree to tree!

'Just as I thought!' thundered Footy Boote. 'It is a combination of a total eclipse of the sun with an unprecedented display of St Elmo's Fire! I knew, of course, that such a coincidence occurs roughly every eighteen thousand years, but it had quite slipped my mind that today was the day!'

His words had risen to a bellow to make them audible above the penetrating shrieks of the terrified savages! For those fellows were certainly not staying around, succulent

r or no succulent white dinner! By the time the
l passed, their panic-stricken canoes were no
paddling dots on the brightening horizon!

exclaimed Beaky, 'that was a pretty close shave,
eh, s.

Footy Boote plucked a still glowing ember from a
lightning-struck tree, and lit his pipe with a steady hand.

'A great Englishman once had a word for it, Beaky,' he
murmured, blowing a smoke ring and calmly watching it
dissolve in the clear afternoon air. 'He, unless I am very
much mistaken, would have described it as a damned
close-run thing!'

Tell Me, Vladimir Ilyich, Are There Any More at Home Like You?

LENIN'S ear has fallen off.

This is not a clue to fourteen across. Neither is it the plangent refrain of an SS nursery rhyme, nor a graffito sprayed onto the west face of County Hall by drunken Sloanes.

It is not even a monitory cryptogram morsed to Palace Gate in the still watches of the night, advising their blue-chinned tweenies to bung a few things in an Aeroflot hold-all and make for Heathrow on account of activities not compatible with light housework only.

It is a fact. It was in the *Sunday Telegraph.* A British tourist, filing past the extremely late V.I. Ulyanov, noticed that the great embalmee was conspicuously monaural. Sixty-one years, it would seem, had wrought their dreadful toll. So, circumspectly resisting, no doubt, the temptation to make the mausoleum ring with yet another rewrite of *Colonel Bogey,* the tourist ran off instead, and told the *Telegraph.*

Clearly, there is food for thought here, but let us not snatch and gobble. This stuff must marinate. Apart from anything else, the incident has to be seen, as you will already have guessed, in the light of the Common Frog and the 1985 engagement book of a man garrotted in Cheshire four hundred years before the birth of Brutus.

Obvious explanations of Lenin's grievous loss will not do at all. Had the ear, for example, merely detached itself through natural process (hastened, possibly, by the reverberant passage outside of ICBM's on May Day rehearsal), it would have dropped to the bottom of the coffin, been retrieved by a weeping daily, and respectfully nailed back on. But, according to the *Telegraph,* it is not there at all.

Nor, surely, can it have been nicked by a souvenir hunter. Even had he been able to lift the glass lid without being perforated by an invigilating Kalashnikov, would he not have been aware of the likely penalty – in a country where pocketing a beer-mat carries a minimum ten-year stretch in the Lubyanka – of being found in possession of a star organ?

Yet more unthinkable is the offchance that the ear was stolen for gain. We know, of course, that there is a thriving market in antique bits—only two years since, you may recall, Napoleon Bonaparte's winkle came up, as it were, at auction, tastefully boxed, *In Fair Condition For Its Year, Formerly The Property Of A Gentleman,* and fetched £20,000 —but they require a legal provenance. No dealer in the world would touch a bent ear, it would be harder to fence than the Mona Lisa. Interpol would be all over his premises before he had the tinfoil off.

There is thus no question but that the ear has been premeditatedly removed by the authorities.

What is removing the Common Frog, on the other hand, is less clear. By one of those joyful serendipities with which zoology is rife, the catalogue moniker of the Common Frog is *Rana temporaria*, and that, sadly, is what it is rapidly demonstrating itself to be. According to, this time, *The Guardian,* opinion is in a shambles: some say it is down to pesticides, some that the blame lies with predatory petshops, some believe it is a new strain of carnivorous mallard, some attribute the disaster to an as yet unidentified frogicidal bacterium, but whatever the cause, the ponds of the queendom are approaching froglessness at a tragic and terrifying rate. Scan the scum and no eyes blink back. Scan the banks, and nothing is hopping about. Cock an ear in vain for plop and croak. The frog is vanishing. Daphnae are baffled.

Help, however, is at hand. But it is, even more however, controversial help, the sort of help which brings clerics fulminating to their pulpits, and postmen cursing to the front door of *The Times* and bannered petitioners shrieking to Downing Street and wholefood dingbats in Sellotaped spectacles to the studios of Channel Four, because it is help construed as flying in the face of nature or God, or both.

For the plan is not to ban pesticides, burn down petshops, wean the mallard onto cheeseburgers, or devise a two-bob tonic that the frog can take twice a day after meals. The plan is to build frogs.

Now, oddly enough, this solution would come as no

surprise at all to a man born 2,500 years ago in Cheshire, although not dug up until last summer. He was found to be dead, but this did not prevent his appearing on television a fortnight back, in his own show. Wogan could learn a lot.

Pete Marsh, as some archaeological wag had dubbed him, was in remarkably good nick. He had, for example, both ears, which gave him a thick edge over Lenin, albeit they were the colour and size of a kipper, as the result of his head having been flattened by the pressure of the peat bog under which he had whiled away the previous twenty-five centuries. His legs had gone a bit small, too, as they would. He also had a stomach where Lenin has sawdust, now the size and consistency of a finger-stall, true, yet containing enough mummified breakfast for experts in this arcane hobby to reveal that he had recently been eating toast.

But you know experts. Never satisfied. Having gleaned all they can from this wrinkled homunculus, they now wish to discover how he was in life, what he looked like, how he voted, and could he bowl a true googly or was it just a bump in the pitch? To this end, they have scalpelled a sliver of tissue from his hapless residue, and embarked it upon an extremely unsettling course.

They are going to clone him. They are going to take his cell-signature, subject it to whatever necromantic bombardments they have come up with in their terrible basements, and reconstruct the Missing Toastivore exactly as he was in life. He will, though, not contain the *breath* of life. There are no plans, as far as I am aware, to get him walking down to Waitrose for a Wonderloaf, despite the keen anthropological interest as to whether he prefers his toast tan or crunchy. Not that they could not do it if they really put their minds to it, it is simply that, if they did, a mob of villagers would burst in and chuck Igor off the battlements.

Because it is do-able. It has been done. And it is about to be done again with the only species where experiments have been successful: the Common — you guessed? — Frog. For that is the solution which has been mooted to offset the sunset of *Rana temporaria:* clone them in vitro, in their tens of thousands, and let them loose.

What else remains for us, but to assemble two and two?

In Russia, there are no prissy strictures against offending God or Fleet Street. There is no electorate to wreak its cyclic penalty. If you've got the hat with the feather in, you can do what you like.

They have had a couple of tough years in the Praesidium. These days, delivery boys whistle martial music, just to be on the safe side. It is bad news, because when monoliths wobble, cracks begin to appear all over the place.

They are running out of praesidual timber. Should Gorbachov in his turn, succumb to croup, they'll probably have to advertise.

Unless the new scheme works.

The ear will be somewhere deep in the Urals by now, in a snug cruiseproof bunker, with eight eminences in white coats standing around its tureen of formaldehyde, watching the tiny bubbles rise from the attached filaments as computers whirr and bright diodes wink and a faint, possible sulphurous, odour makes the nostrils twitch.

If it works with frogs and ancient corpses, why could it not work with Lenin? He was, after all, the best and the brightest, he came in, waving, on a train once, why could he not do so again, and again, and again?

They'll have to get the technology right, mind. If he hops off the cow-catcher and goes 'Rivet-rivet! Rivet-rivet!', anyone owning the Czar's ear could well be in with a chance.

An Article About . . .

Volunteers who fear they may be losing their memories are being sought by Professor Patrick Rabbitt of Manchester University for research into absent-mindedness.

Daily Telegraph

August the, the

Dear Professor Rabbitt,

I do hope you will forgive my writing to you out of the, without prior, out of the, we have not met, but I saw the item in the *Daily,* blue, but I saw your item in the *Sunday,* in the, I heard the item on the car, unless it was *News at,* um, you see a picture of Old Ben, the big hand is on the, on the, or to put it another way, the liittle hand is, the little hand is, anyhow you hear the pips, the chimes, and they go one, two, three, God Almighty, do you know, Geoff, I have been watching that programme for the past, for the past, since we lived in, since we lived at number, since we, large block of flats, next to the, small block of flats, next to the Tube, at, at, there was a Sainsbury's across the, there was a Sainsbury's on the corner.

Or a Tesco's.

My wife will remember. She's out in the, she's up on the.

Right, I'm back now, sorry about that, I asked her, and she says I left them on the, on the, they had fallen down behind the, hang on, here's a turn-up for the, for the, on second thoughts I don't think, for the book, I don't think these are mine at all, I always smoke, I have always smoked, purple packet, you must know their advertisement I think there's a pyramid in it, I'm sure there's a pyramid. Or a swan. I pass that ad every morning on my way to, it's as you come down past the, past where that factory used to be with the two big concrete cats outside, its not a factory any more, it's, it's, there was some kind of row about the cats, it's all coming back to me, they had a preservation order on them, they were definitely major cats, the sculptor was a household, I think it's the same man who did the statue of, word, the statue in Thing Square, it isn't Cadogan, square with two syllables, the factory got sold in, got sold some time ago, and didn't someone knock the head off one of the, or were they dogs?

They made biscuits, as I recollect.

If they made biscuits, there would not be cats outside, you do not have cat biscuits. Our cat Timmy never, to my certain knowledge, our cat Percy, never touched anything but, Timmy was the hamster. Timmy was the gerbil.

I think we had two gerbils, I think the gerbils were Gert and Daisy. The hamster was called, Wetherby Terrace is where the factory was. Wetherby Crescent.

I know these are not my cigarettes, there is nothing written on the packet, there was a phone number written on *my* packet, I recall that very clearly, I had to ring someone back, I was drinking a cup of coffee when he rang, I walked to the telephone, I said Hallo, and he said Hallo, it's, and he said Hallo, it's.

Gert and Daisy were the goldfish.

Fortunately, there is no problem here. If I go and make another cup of coffee and walk over to the telephone again it will come back to me, I will recall his name in a, it is all a question of retracing one's, of reconstructing, in a flash, it is an infallible method of, steps.

No problem! Never fails!

The gerbils were called Benson and Hedges.

I knew it the moment I pulled the chain.

As far as the square is concerned all I have to do is hold the sound of the two syllables in my head, Donk-donk Square, and then I imagine the red-brick wall at a height of about, what, fifteen feet, and I gradually work my way round it until I come to the place on the wall where the name is, because I have driven round it umpteen times, and I have actually seen the name up there. Due to the one-way system, you have to go through Donk-donk Square if you want to get from, from, that's to say if you want to get into, if you want to drive between one place and another, or here's another good way of remembering the name. I start with the statue which was done by the same man, incidentally, who did the dogs outside the former biscuit factory in, in, the former biscuit factory near the advert for the cigarettes I always smoke, why am I holding this coffee cup, and if I imagine myself driving past the statue on my right, a man on a horse, as I recall, then the square-name is just visible under the arm he is raising his hat with.

Donk-donk Square.

It could be you have to imagine driving past the statue on your left.

Another quick way would be to look the man up in a book about statues in London squares. He would be easy to identify because the statue is almost certainly a twentieth-century statue, as the sculptor did the dogs as well, and they did not make biscuits in factories prior to 1900, I am certain I heard that somewhere, and if you took that as your starting point in the library, i.e. statues of men on horses put up after 1900, then it would be a matter of minutes, once you had got your library ticket from the safe place you always keep it.

However, to get to the, to tackle the main, to, good God, it's just occurred to me that the Tesco's was not on the corner, if it was a Tesco's opposite the block of flats where we had our first telly and watched whatever it was, the Tesco's was on the corner opposite where we moved to in 19, in 19, there was a petrol shortage and I think Adam Faith sang *O Mein Gerbil,* was it, or could it have been Dickie Valentine, alternatively does the name John F. Nasser strike a familiar note? Somebody with a moustache and a striking resemblance to, oh Jesus, tall offspin bowler, Gordon, Gordon, Gordon something.

Anyway, if that is where the Tesco's was in fact opposite, i.e. the little terraced house in, in, call it Donk-donk-donk Avenue for the time being, we can come back to that, it had two gravel bins at one end, I have the feeling the man who phoned this morning would remember, I can't exactly put my finger on why, it is a vague feeling I have he was a close relative, a father for example, but in that case why did I write down his phone number, I know my father's phone number like the back of my, of my, it could always be he was phoning from somewhere else, hand, did it have something to do with coffee? Anyway, if that is where the Tesco's was in fact opposite, that would not have been where I first saw that, that, concrete dog advert, was it, because we brought the television with us from the flat that wasn't anywhere with a Tesco's on the corner opposite, so whatever it was I saw, I didn't see it there.

I'm glad that's settled.

Which leaves me with, I think, only one question unanswered. I have just read through this letter again, Professor Rabbitt, and it appears to have been written to you.

I do not know you from bloody, from bloody, the name

means nothing, Adam. You're not the person who phoned me this morning, by any chance?

And if it's about my library ticket, I'd like it back as soon as possible.

What's your address?

Vox Populi, Vox Dei

According to the new Bishop of Bristol, one positive result of the Bishop of Durham controversy was that people were now talking about God in pubs.

Daily Telegraph

'IF HE came back,' said the man in the herringbone overcoat, 'if He came in here now, as I understand is on the cards, theologically speaking, if He came prancing in here right this minute, what would you say to Him?'

'First off,' replied the man in the QPR scarf, dabbing its fringe delicately across his lagered lip, 'first off, He would not prance. He is meek and mild, according to informed sources, and the meek and mild do not prance.'

'They inherit the earth,' said the bearded man confidently, 'it's all coming back to me.'

'Only the meek,' said the man in the herringbone overcoat, 'Probably the meek and powerful. The meek and mild get sod all, I have seen 'em in here of an evening, they cannot even get near the bar, they do not even inherit a small sherry.'

'*He* did all right,' countered the QPR supporter quickly. 'He was meek *and* mild, and it never did Him any harm, ask anyone, He has got churches all over with His name up, also millions of books sold, He is another Adrian Mole.'

'He does all right *now*,' said the man in the herringbone overcoat, 'but at the time, if you cast your mind back, He was nailed up, largely due to being meek and mild. If he had been meek and powerful, e.g. Frank Bruno, He would have taken a few of the buggers with him, there would've been Romans lying around all over the shop. You can push the meek and powerful just so far.'

'Would He come in through the wall?' enquired the bearded man.

'What?'

'They do that,' said the bearded man.

'Not if they're Holy ones,' said the QPR supporter. 'It puts people off. Take Abbott and Costello, I have seen

53

their hats fly up in the air. It did not, as I recall, occur to them to fall down before it and praise its name.'

'What I would say to Him,' said a small pallid man who had been thinking deeply but had not yet spoken, 'is *I will have a large Bells and water, if it's all the same to You*. I understand money is no object where He is concerned, He would not think twice, He would probably throw in a packet of pork scratchings, if I know Him.'

'As He has got the knack of turning water into wine,' said the QPR supporter, 'it is on the cards He would not even have to put His hand in His pocket. He would just say something of the order of *Let there be a large Bells*, and there would be a large Bells.'

'Lo,' corrected the man in the herringbone overcoat.

'What?'

'And Lo! there would be a large Bells.'

'Does He do pork scratchings?' said the small pallid man.

The man in the herringbone overcoat drained his glass slowly.

'The phrase *Let there be pork scratchings* does not exactly spring to mind,' he said, 'doubtless due to the fact that there is nothing inferior to a pork scratching for them to be turned into it from.'

The four pondered this for a while. Finally, the QPR supporter said:

'He probably wouldn't recognise it after, what is it, two thousand years? He has probably never seen eleven different kinds of lager, there was probably only mild and bitter in His day.'

'Or meek and bitter, possibly,' said the bearded man.

'As the Prince of Peace,' said the QPR supporter thoughtfully, 'He would probably not go a bundle on electronic games. He would probably come straight through the wall and hang one on that bugger with the tattooed hooter.'

'Tut, tut,' said the man in the herringbone overcoat, shaking his head, 'we have already debated the point about whether He would lash out or not. I thought that was settled. He would merely stroll across and murmur *Arise, take up thy Space Invader machine, and sod off*.'

The small man, who had been meticulously gaffing a crisp-shard from his Guinness with a pencil, now murmured: 'The reason He did not bring up pork scratchings in the Bible is probably due to where they were against His religion.'

'They are not against His religion *now,*' said the bearded man. 'He has adapted it in His infinite wisdom to take account of pig products.'

'You can resist bacon for just so long' said the man in the herringbone overcoat. 'I have been on a diet and I speak as one who knows. No one could be expected to hold out for two thousand years, it is more than human flesh and blood could stand. Or,' he added, 'anything else.'

'They could've had chicken scratchings,' said the small man, removing the crisp-shard from his pencil-point, carefully. 'That would have fallen within the Hebrew remit. They get through a lot of chicken, it is a well-known fact.'

The QPR supporter got up, went to the bar, bought another round, returned, set down the four glasses, and said:

'If He drinks.'

The bearded man flinched.

'If He *drinks?*' he cried.

'I got an enamel tray from Viareggio one year,' said the man in the herringbone overcoat, firmly, 'with the last dinner on it.'

'What did you have?' enquired the QPR supporter.

'Not my last dinner, you prat,' said the man in the herringbone overcoat, '*The* Last Dinner. A picture of it. They are all tucking in, and He is in the middle, and they all have goblets. You cannot tell me it is water. First off, you cannot trust the water out there, second off, we have already debated about where He waves His wand and Lo! a couple of crates of red.'

'That was *then,*' countered the bearded man, 'while He was still in a position to get legless, i.e. prior to rising again. There cannot be much in a quick half for Him these days.'

'It saves us the embarrassment of buying Him a round,' said the small pallid man. 'I for one would have a job saying *What's yours, O Lord?*'

The other three nodded, this clearly having been something that had long been lying at the back of their minds.

'Nor,' said the man in the herringbone overcoat,

eructating with more than usual respect, 'would I fancy the landlord's job, come three o'clock.'

'Come along, O Lord, finish up, if you please,' muttered the bearded man.

'Exactly,' said the man in the herringbone overcoat. *'Time, O Lord, please,* and bunging a wet bar-cloth at Him if He did not shift.'

The QPR supporter brightened.

'It could be that He would be in a position to change the licensing laws if He came again,' he said. 'I think They can do that. I seem to remember reading somewhere about what a Supreme Being is entitled to do.'

'No,' said the main in the herringbone overcoat sharply, 'you are definitely out of order there. There's that stuff about Him taking out a two-bob bit and pointing out that it is up to Caesar to fix the licensing laws, speed limits, whether clockwork toys carry VAT etcetera etcetera. Come closing-time, He would be mooning about in the car-park with the rest of us, wondering whether to go and get some Chinese takeaway.'

The small pallid man sniffed cracklingly.

'There's another thing,' he said. 'You couldn't tell Him any jokes.'

'I don't follow,' said the QPR supporter.

'He is omniwossname,' said the small pallid man. 'He has got all jokes in His head, along with times of the last buses and so forth. You would say *Have You heard the one about. . .* and that would be as far as you got.'

A somewhat glum silence followed this.

'I suppose,' said the bearded man, after a reflective minute or two, 'He's a dab hand at darts, as well.'

'Not necessarily,' replied the man in the herringbone overcoat brightening. 'There is, as far as I am aware, nothing in the Bible about Him and darts. Or, now I think about it, dominoes.'

'Get off!' snapped the QPR supporter. '(a) He has had ample opportunity to practise over the past two thousand years, never mind (b), you cannot tell me He is going to go to all the trouble of a Second Coming only to put Himself in the position of getting seen off by Jocky Wilson. It would do no good at all to the credibility of a Supreme Being, getting stuck on double one all night.'

'Also,' said the small pallid man, 'if He came on Amateur

topless Go-Go Evening, we could well be into a wet blanket situation. Speaking for myself, I would definitely hold back from poking a folded Newton into anything spangled.'

'That big wall-eyed one from Clapham,' mumured the QPR supporter, nodding gloomily, 'ends up in nothing but a chocolate crucifix. I can see trouble there.'

The man in the herringbone overcoat sucked his teeth and released a long glum exhalation.

'All in all,' he said, 'I do not relish this prospect one little bit.'

'Still,' said the QPR supporter, 'look on the bright side. The Bishop of thing, Durham, reckons it is all a load of old codswollop, there is no question of Anybody coming back anywhere, never did, never will.'

The small pallid man snorted.

'Fat lot he knows,' he said.

Grey Area

Most of the red squirrels released experimentally into Regent's Park have survived the winter in fine form, London Zoo said yesterday. Of the ten animals released in stages last October, seven are known to have survived in good health. One was killed by a car, one by a feral cat, and one, whose radio collar failed, has not been seen for several weeks.

Red squirrels have been supplanted throughout most of Britain by the Grey species. The Times

IT BEING, finally, Spring, and I a victim, willy-nilly, of verbal propaganda, I not only dug, but whistled as I dug.

I had turned two beds to the texture of cold Christmas pudding, and was about to jab the spade into the third, beneath the bare acacia tree, when a voice said:

'If you want to hear *Rigoletto* murdered, you could not have come to a better place.'

I dropped the spade. A robin, no less startled, coughed out a haunch of worm and shot off, like a feathered bullet.

The voice had come from above my head. I glanced carefully upward, tensed for an arboreal mugger; mine is a neighbourhood rife with inventive villainy. But there was nothing in the acacia save two squirrels, one grey, and one, remarkably, red. I was about to put the voice down to something carried on a freak of breeze when the red squirred cocked its little head towards the grey and said:

'Not, of course, that I am a fan of the early Verdi. Ripeness did not touch him until *Otello*.'

'I'll take your word for it,' said the grey squirrel. 'Personally, I stop at Dennis Lotis.'

The honest sweat formed icicles beneath my arms.

'You speak English,' I heard myself say.

'Alternatively,' said the red, 'you would appear to have a grasp of basic squirrel.'

'Nice one, Quentin,' said the grey.

'Forgive me,' I said, 'I have never heard a squirrel talk before.'

The red squirrel scuttled along its bough, and down the trunk until its currant eye was level with my own.

'That,' it said sharply, 'is because you have only come across greys, with whom you have nothing in common.'

'Our only wossname, interest,' said the grey, 'is nuts. Cob, hazel, acorn, you name it. I could tell you stories about nuts what'd make your hair stand on end, only what's the point?'

'They are a simple folk,' said his colleague.

'Watch it,' said the grey.

'But fundamentally decent,' said the red quickly. 'They have been gravely misrepresented.'

'I blame the media,' said the grey. 'I have heard the word rat mentioned on several occasions. Also, a lot of old codswallop about goldtops and cream sucked out. Personally, I never touch the stuff, it makes you run, cream.'

I moved, a shade unsteadily, to a garden bench, and sat down. They followed, sharing a corroded roller, and watched me.

'Have you been to the Chagall?' enquired the red. 'Primitive psycho-drama it may be, but there is no denying that for sheer luminescent colour, he had no—'

'Forgive me for interrupting,' I said striving to restrain the tell-tale wobble of my cigarette smoke, 'but I had always understood that grey and red squirrels did not, er, get on. Indeed, I rather thought that it was the grey squirrel that was primarily responsible for decimating the red.'

'The happiest nations have no history,' murmured the red squirrel. 'I have always been particularly partial to George Eliot's delicate ironies.'

'I could listen to him talk all day,' said the grey.

'We have put the past behind us,' said the red.

'Definitely,' said the grey. 'I am his minder. He would be the first to admit he cannot look after hisself. His mate got turned over by a *cat!* I do cats as a matter of course, just to keep my claw in; I got four toms one morning, it looked like Nagasaki outside my dray, it's all a question of the throat. His brother copped it from a green Volvo, didn't he?'

'He stopped in the middle of Regent's Park Road,' said the red, glumly, 'in order to work out a geotropic crux.'

'They prised him out of the tyre treads just this side of Runcorn,' said the grey squirrel, 'as I understand it. Reds may be dab hands at Latin etcetera, but the Green Cross

Code is a closed book to 'em. Without me, he'd be gravy on a gypsy's lip, wouldn't you, Quentin?'

'*Chacun à son métier,*' said the red.

'Hear that?' cried the grey, proudly. 'You could take him anywhere!'

I cleared my throat.

'It's coming back to me now,' I said. 'There was an item in *The Times;* you must be the one whose radio collar failed?'

The tiny head nodded jerkily.

'It was quite frightful, I found myself picking up *My Word!*'

'I had to gnaw it off him,' affirmed the grey, 'he was belting round in circles, he was turning somersaults, he could've done hisself a mischief.'

'I simply cannot stand Frank Muir,' said the red squirrel, a shiver rippling its russet pelt. 'If I want fake Edwardiana, I go to Waring & Gillow.'

The grey squirrel bared its yellow fangs, and let a rodent chuckle slip.

'He could have his own show, am I right?' he said. 'Quick as a flash, and subtle, too. He could run rings round Wogan. Don't talk to me about dolphins!'

'What?' I said.

'Dolphins. Big wet buggers like a long inner tube, silly bloody grin all the time, they are supposed to be clever, they do not hold a candle to your red squirrel.'

'Nor the grey,' said his friend, warmly. 'I should like to see a dolphin handle an acorn.'

'I have certain manual wossnames, true,' murmured the grey, shyly.

'You seem,' I said, 'to have an exceptional *rapport.*'

'True,' replied the red. 'Of course, as you have adumbrated, it was not ever thus. My dear chum here would be the first to admit that what might be termed Grey Power stood until very recently in grave danger of taking over Great Britain completely.'

'He is not wrong,' said the grey. 'It is what Klagenfuhrt described as the tyranny of the simple.'

'I say!' I cried.

'Yes,' said the red squirrel, happily, 'he *is* rather coming along, isn't he?'

'Thanks to you, Quentin,' replied the grey warmly. It

turned once more to me. 'Up until recently, I could not do *No Litter. No Bicycles. Dogs Must Be Kept On A Lead* without touching each word with my conk and moving my lips, but I am now fair whipping through the stuff! Where was I? Oh yes, grey squirrels driving out the red, brute force and mindlessness in the name of the bogus democracy of the unlettered masses, conspicuous socio-political reduction to the lowest common denominator, plus rooted traditional bigotry against elitism, i.e. get off my acorn, you pouf, or I will have your tripes out—yes, I am afraid Great Britain was definitely going down the tubes, squirrel-wise!'

The red squirrel sighed.

> *'Milton! Thou shouldst be living at this hour:*
> *England hath need of thee; she is a fen of stagnant waters.'*

The grey squirrel sucked its honed canines admiringly.

'Quentin has one for every occasion,' he said.

It was my turn, now, to sigh.

'I am deeply impressed,' I said. 'I had believed that the red squirrel would be torn limb from limb in Regent's Park. I had not dared to hope for reconciliation, nay, for mutual assistance and shared skills, for co-operation and understanding between you.'

'I like the way he said *nay* ,' said the grey squirrel. 'He is a toff.'

'There are no toffs!' snapped the red squirrel. 'We have eliminated class.'

'It is just an expression,' murmured the grey squirrel.

'I am stirred,' I said, for I was.

'I follow you,' said the red squirrel gently. 'Two legs bad, four legs good.'

'You've bloody lost me, now,' said the grey.

The red squirrel took up a declamatory position on its hindpaws, and said:

> *'One impulse from a vernal wood*
> *Can teach you more of man;*
> *Of moral evil and of good,*
> *Than all the sages can.'*

The grey squirrel beamed.

'Wordsworth,' he said.

IN 986 THE MANOR OF HAMPSTEAD
WAS GRANTED BY KING ETHELRED
TO THE MONKS OF WESTMINSTER

IN 1986 WE CELEBRATE 1000 YEARS
OF COMMUNITY AND CHURCH

THIS LEAFLET HAS BEEN DONATED AND PRINTED BY
PIP PRINTING LTD. 166 WEST END LANE. NW6 TEL: 794 7858
PIP for Printing and Copying with service!
We're years ahead of the rest!

986 Monks of Westminster granted Manor of Hampstead. Nuns of Westminster demand name be changed to Personor of Hampstead, set up Ad Hoc Sisterhood Consciousness Protest Solidarity Committee, burn wimples, learn judo. Hampstead Battered Nun Refuge founded by Sister Erin, Mother Vastly Superior.

988 Flaske Walke man paints front gate blue. Hampstead Conservation Society founded. Man hung, drawn, and quartered. Gate restored.

991 Battle of Maldon: overwhelming defeat of Byrhtnoth of Essex by Viking insurgents. This totally unexpected disaster due entirely to march to Maldon Common site by Hampstead Campaign for Broadsword Disarmament, who, according to report in *Anglo-Saxon Chronicle*, "climbed ye shieldwalle and sette up a grete clamor amung ye byrhnothshoop, sum sange we shall over-

cum But otheres of thir numbre wyshinge to sing we shal notte Bee mooved attaked them and much Blode was shedde Betweene ye two factions, in ye confusion, ye vykynges fel upon Byrhnoth's force and slewe them.'

1000 Leif Ericsson discovers North America. Hampstead Conservation Society mounts **no junkfoode litter here** rally. Many dead.

1016 Cnut becomes King of England. Hampstead Council For Environmental Concern protests at threat of shoreline erosion. Graffiti campaign: '**silly cnut**' appears all over Hampstead walls. Walls immediately demolished by Hampstead Wimmin For Direct Action Now.

1066 Norman invasion by William the Bastard. All England rises in arms, except for Hampstead. Hampstead Single Parents Solidarity Workshop marches to Hastings, attacks Harold's army from rear. Harold defeated.

1067 England's first *Cuisine Normande* restaurant opened in Heath Street. Adrian the Svelte does the cooking and his friend Pippin the Trick waits on tables. Speciality: mince.

1086 domesday Boke published. Launch party thrown at Flaske Walke Bokeshop by Boker Prize Committee. Disappointment expressed that Domesday Boke is written in Latin, on grounds that language not obscure enough. Boker Prize awarded to stick with Maori runes on it.

1099 First Crusade under command of Geoffrey of Bouillon takes Jerusalem. All England rejoices, except for Hampstead. Hampstead CBD sets up *Crusaders Out!* campaign, calling for immediate unconditional talks on a united Palestine and the release of all Provisional Saracens held under the emergency regulations.

1100 William Rufus killed while hunting in New Forest. All England mourns, except for Hampstead. Hampstead Vegans Of Diminished Height Against Blood Sports organise week-long street festival, including mock coronation of cabbage.

1215 King John signs magna carta, in High Hille Bokeshop. Last-minute clause inserted by barons gives them 15% on all sales over first ten thousand, plus 50% of vellumback rights.

1290 Expulsion of Jews by Edward I. Collapse of Hampstead house prices.

1327 Deposition and murder of Edward II at Berkeley Castle. All England says about bloody time, him and his poof gaveston, what is this countrie cumming to? except Hampstead, which announces week of mourning, everyone wears black, set off by just a touch of discreet pastel colour at the collar and cuffs.

1338 Beginning of Hundred Years' Stop The War Rally.

1349 Black Death strikes England, bringing grief, terror, misery, and, in Hampstead, extreme annoyance. Residents refuse to pay rates until local health authority agrees to drop the work *black*.

1381 Peasants' Revolt. Not surprisingly, this is an immediate runaway success with Hampstead's broad left. just smocks opens in Heath Street, playne cookynge on an appallingly tinie agricultural wage goes to four editions, and some eight hundred well-born Hampstead ladies run off with swineherds, many of them with the same man due to severe swineherd shortage.

1400 Owen Glendower revolts in Wales. Hampstead enters a week's state mourning for incinerated weekend cottages.

1476 Caxton sets up first printing press. 93% of Hampstead population send him manuscript novels about marital disharmony.

1477 Battle of Nancy: defeat and death of Charles the Bold spells collapse of Burgundy. News shrugged off by Hampstead, where everyone prefers very drinkable unpretentious Lapp hock from wonderful little man round corner.

1536 Execution of Anne Boleyn brings Hampstead to brink of civil war. Abolitionists (Fight The Cuts!) clash with supporters of Henry VIII (Quickie Divorces Now!), as Lesbians For A Saner World launch furious attack on Wonderful Huge Families All Sharing A Hot Tub Is The Only Way campaigners. Fashionable pacifism finally prevails, but does not prevent skirmishes continuing for the next four centuries.

1558 Calais lost by English to French. All England weeps, except for Hampstead, where opinion is that cheese will improve.

1588 Armada defeated. All England cheers, except for Hampstead, where opinion is that olive oil will vanish.

1605 Gunpowder Plot. Petition to release Guy Fawkes got up by Concerned Hampstead Anti-Firework Mums For A More Caring Society.

1616 Death of Shakespeare. 'OVER-RATED'—*Hampstead & Highgate Expresse.*

1649 Execution of Charles I brings fierce protest from Hampstead, since establishment of Commonwealth means theatres will shut.

1660 Restoration of Charles II, on the other hand, brings deep (but unspoken) misery to Hampstead, since it means theatres will open again and—having kicked up so much fuss in 1649—they will now have to start going.

1710 First Tory Government in Britain. First case of schizophrenia in Hampstead.

1750 Death of J.S. Bach, giving whole of Hampstead wonderful opportunity to point out he was not a patch on W.F. Bach, K.P.E. Bach, J.C.B. Bach, or, indeed, Sugar Ray Bach, the Leipzig cruiserweight.

1785 Edmund Cartwright invents power loom, to wretchedness of Hampstead citizenry who recognise that Sunday mornings will never be same again, now that designer sweaters accessible to *hoi polloi*. Half-hearted specious attempt by Friends Of The Sheep to thwart mass-production stoutly repulsed by jubilant Coney Liberation Front, who see loom as death-knell of rodent chic.

1805 Flags fly at half-mast for Horatio Nelson, patron saint of Hampstead Disabled Adulterers Collective.

1815 Exiled dissident Napoleon Bonaparte becomes focus of Save The St Helena One campaign, which urges sacrifice and self-denial. Hampstead courageously refuses to drink British sherry, eat British citrus fruits, patronise British bullfights, buy British pasta, watch British opera, wear British diamonds, or take British holidays.

1825 World's first railway opened between Stockton and Darlington. Received by rest of Britain as great leap forward, it is immediately boycotted by Hampstead until such time as satisfactory guarantees can be given concerning pollution, noise, military potential, smell, jobs, property values, threats to Heath wildlife, carriage of harmful waste, and rape in tunnels.

1834 Launch of the heavily supported Help A Tolpuddle Martyr By Buying His Cottage And Gentrifying It Scheme.

1883 Death of Marx causes widespread local shock: Hampstead Militants For A Bigger Slice Of The Tourist Cake lead protest march to Highgate Cemetery in attempt to get Marx exhumed and reburied in Hampstead.

1909 Blériot crash-lands in Dover after first cross-Channel flight. Ecstatic crowds flock to welcome him. Hampstead man pokes about in wreckage for Beaujolais Nouveau.

1914–1918 Great Book Shortage.

1924 Ramsay MacDonald becomes first Labour Prime Minister, causing enormous excitement among Hampstead socialist intellectuals. Dozens of cells immediately set up to discuss movement of assets to Zurich.

1928 First talkie: *The Jazz Singer*. Huge public meetings on Hampstead Heath to discuss sub-text of *Climb Upon My Knee, Sonny Boy*. 3 killed, 17 injured, in riots over quality of second-unit direction.

1938 Freud leaves Vienna, arrives in Hampstead. Woken on first morning by 34,000 local patients queueing in road outside.

1948 Post-Second Great Book Shortage housing boom heralds rise of Hampstead as colonial power. Several hundred estate carpetbaggers move into Hampstead, set up agency tents, begin redrawing map: Hampstead borders now embrace Swiss Cottage, Belsize Park, Childs Hill, Fortune Green, Chalk Farm, Cricklewood. Annexation of Sudetenland not ruled out.

1966 Slim, elegant, impossibly handsome humorous hack buys house in Hampstead. Immediately informed by Hampstead well-wishers two hundred yards West that house in Swiss Cottage, actually.

1972 Hack sells house in Swiss Cottage Actually. Moves to Hampstead. Immediately informed by Hampstead well-wishers two hundred yards East that house in Cricklewood, actually.

1986 1000th anniversary of Hampstead. Own back got by man in Cricklewood Actually.

MR NOON

by D.H. Lawrence

A Novel by D.H. Lawrence is to be published by Cambridge University Press next month, 54 years after his death. Researchers found the MS. among papers at the Humanities Research Centre of the University of Texas, Austin.

The new book is called 'Mr Noon.' Lawrence wrote it in two parts and hoped they would be published as separate novels, but the publishers found them too short.

Daily Telegraph.

MR NOON lived up to his name.

He did not get up with the cock.

He did not get up with the sun.

He did not get up and collect the nice fat heavy eggs, still warm from squeezing out of the plump chicken loins.

He did not get up and tug the long rubbery-flubbery teats of Daisy the Cow so that the bright hot milk spurted ringingly into the big dark depths of the bucket.

He did not get up and take Roger the Ram down to the bleating sheep to let Roger the Ram go humpity-humpity and make the sheep feel as if great big waves were crashing on the shore time and time and time again.

Mr Noon did not get up in the morning at all.

He stayed in his bed until noon.

Mr Noon would stay in his bed in case a visitor turned up.

Many visitors *did* turn up at the little cottage, but Mr Noon would send them away again.

Every day, the Postman would call up to the little open window of Mr Noon's bedroom.

'Good morning, Mr Noon!'

And every day, Mr Noon would call out:

'Eff off, Postman!'

Every day, the Jehovah's Witness would call up to the little open window of Mr Noon's bedroom.

'Good morning, Mr Noon!'

And every day, Mr Noon would call out:

'Eff off, Jehovah's Witness!'

And so on.

Mr Noon liked using naughty words. He did not think they were naughty at all, and he was right. People who object to naughty words are guilty of hypocrisy and cant. Mr Noon hated cant.

'Silly cant!' said Mr Noon, lying in his bed.

He would look at the ceiling all morning, and make pictures in his head. Don't you do that, too?

Mr Noon would see trains rushing into long dark tunnels.

'Whoosh!' went the trains.

'Wheeee!' went their whistles, inside the tunnels.

Mr Noon would see his Dad going to work.

His Dad was a miner. Every day, his Dad went down a long dark hole. When he got to the bottom, he would take out his big shovel.

Dig, dig, dig, went Dad Noon!

Mr Noon would see all this, lying on his bed.

He would also see his Mum. Mum Noon was a schoolteacher. But most of all, she liked riding horses. He would see her, on the ceiling, riding a big black stallion, with her skirt tucked into her knickers, and her nostrils flaring. The stallion's nostrils flared, too. Sometimes they would ride into a tunnel, if there wasn't a train coming.

When they got home, they were all sweaty! So Mum Noon would get out a great big tin bath, and put it in front of the fire, and put the horse in it, and scrub its back.

Mr Noon liked that picture best of all.

By mid-day, when no visitors had called, except the Gasman, and the Man About The Rates, and the Double

Glazing Man, and the Reader's Digest Man, and the Tally Man, Mr Noon would at last get out of bed, grind his big yellow teeth, and say:

'Boogger! Boogger! Boogger!'

Then he would clump down the little creaky staircase in his big honest clogs and out into the smelly old farmyard and try to find something nice to worm.

On a good day, it might be Sharon the Sow. But on a bad day, it might only be Corky the Cat.

Then, one fine, ripening, spring morning, with the fat fuzzy pussy-willow catkins jiggling up and down outside his bedroom window and making his throat go all dry and funny, Mr Noon heard an unfamiliar voice call up from below.

'I say!' it trilled. 'Is anyone at home?'

Slowly, the image of tall dark beetling industrial chimneys raping innocent verdant hills faded from Mr Noon's ceiling. The voice was not a Postman's voice or, indeed, anything remotely like it.

'Aye,' grunted Mr Noon cautiously, from the bed (for it was still only ten-fifteen). 'Aye, appen there be.'

'Oh, ripping!' cried the voice. 'Oh, top-hole! Oh, super!'

Slowly Mr Noon broke the habit of a lifetime and, well before mid-day, swung his big hairy feet out of bed and onto the linoleum, and walked, squeak-squeak-squeak, to the little window and looked out.

Mr Noon found himself staring down into the upturned smiling face and almost equally upturned open blouse of a very pretty lady. Mr Noon gripped the little window ledge with his big hairy hands to stop them trembling: it was a Visitor!

'Can ah elp thee, miss?' croaked Mr Noon

'Oh, would you?' cried the young lady. 'I was just driving past in my motor and I could not help noticing your little chickens. I have a teensy-weensy dinner-party tonight, just a few ripping top-hole chums from the upper classes, and a couple of plump pullets would be absolutely tickety-boo!'

Mr Noon closed his eyes. Then he opened them again, struggled to ungrip his hands from the little window ledge, and retreated, lurching, into the room.

Mr Noon pulled on his thick corduroy trousers.

Mr Noon pulled on his coarse linen shirt.

Mr Noon spat on his big hairy hands and smoothed down his big hairy head.

Then he went downstairs. Clump, clump, clump, went his clogs.

Mr Noon stepped into the unfamiliar morning.

'Pullet?' he said, hoarsely.

'Definitely!' trilled the young lady.

The breeze blew her thin cotton skirt against her legs. Her huge eyes were the deep blue of a faceworker's scars. The sun caught her soft forearm down, reminding Mr Noon of the lioness's belly at Nottingham Zoo.

Mr Noon licked his lips.

'Appen ah'll ketch thee a couple,' he murmured, fighting a sudden dizzy spell. 'Tha'll want plump 'uns, ah tek it?'

The young lady nodded, and winked, and clapped her hands, and giggled.

Mr Noon lunged suddenly, his huge corded muscles bulging, and hurled himself at the squawking chickens.

Scuttle! went the chickens.

Grab! went Mr Noon.

Kof-kof-kof! went the chickens.

Oh! went the young lady.

Mr Noon brought them to her, one in each hand. They were still warm. They were still wriggling, slightly. She touched the plump little bodies with her long slim white fingers.

'So many feathers!' she murmured. 'And I'm late already.' She turned her big blue eyes up to Mr Noon's strong dark face. 'I suppose a pluck would be out of the question?' she said.

Mr Noon fainted.

When he came round, he found the Postman, the Double Glazing Man, the Tally Man, the Reader's Digest Man, and the Man About the Rates standing over him. They had been watching, the way folk do in those parts.

Only the Jehovah's Witness had made an excuse and left.

'Where be er?' enquired Mr Noon.

'Er be gone,' replied the Postman.

'Funny to see you up and about so early,' said the Tally Man. 'Reckon as how we won't be able to call you Mr Noon no more.'

The Double Glazing Man nudged him in the ribs, and winked.

'Mister Bloody Good Opportunity, more like!' he said.

How everybody laughed!

All except Mr Noon, of course.

Red Sales in the Sunset

Sun Guiying, a middle-aged woman chicken farmer, was given the full propaganda treatment in China's Press yesterday as a heroine of the new peasant elite. This year she has sold more than 492,800 eggs.

Her family's profit was said to be £12,486 sterling and so she was entitled to the ultimate accolade—she was given permission to become Peking's first peasant to own a car.

Daily Telegraph

A SAFFRON hangnail of moon rose gently over Dao Deng Hua, tinting the corrugated roofs of its serried coops. Inside, ten thousand chickens, ranked like feathered kebabs upon their alloy perches, let out one last staccato choral cluck, and settled, knackered, for the night.

In the village Hall Of Egg Norm Victory And Reciprocal Criticism, five hundred peasants packed the wooden benches no less formally, but far more excitedly: five hundred eager faces shone above the collars of their dropping-spattered smocks, a thousand rapt and gleaming eyes targeted in on the little raised platform, a thousand hands ignored the decadent speculation as to the sound of one of them clapping and set up a keen and rhythmic beat, as the dais party filed up the steps, and took their seats.

Sun Guiying was, naturally, the last. She did not sit. The applause rose to an echoing crescendo, bringing flakes of cheap eau-de-nil distemper fluttering down from the trembling ceiling so that, for a brief time-warped moment, she became a demure virgin in an old T'ang frieze, teased by encircling butterflies.

'We welcome ,' said the Chairman, as the cheering at last died down, 'egg heroine Sun Guiying, who—'

'So sorry to be 47.9 seconds late,' interrupted the heroine, bowing slightly, first to the Chairman, then to the audience, 'but these Toyotas are buggers when it comes to cold starting. If throttle-pedal over-depressed, automatic choke flood carburettor. Soon I chop it in, get Merc 450 SEL, gimme that Stuttgart fuel injection every time!'

Below her, jaws dropped open, the bright eyes glazed.

What hens were these, of which the heroine spake? What was the black smear on her nose? Why, above all, was she wearing string-backed gloves? Faster egg-handling? Anti-beak protection? In the depths of the hall, a small man stood up, shyly, and took off his cap.

'Egg heroine Sun Guiying,' he said, 'we, the comrade-soldier-villagers of Dao Deng Hua, congratulate you on the triumphant sale of 492,800 eggs! What is your expert advice to all those who aspire, humbly, to achieve such figures? Is it a question of enriched grit, or perhaps—'

'Get them to throw in loose covers,' replied Sun Guiying briskly. 'That is my advice. Do not let them fob you off with standard PVC upholstery, you would not believe how your bum slides about when drifting through the Nu Hau Heng roundabout, I bloody nearly wrote her off, there was this yo-yo in a clapped-out Su Shiu 205 tractor, fortunately I was able to take him on the inside, these people should not be allowed on road, also, since you raise question, do not take delivery before they have modified suspension, this is a factory job, the Toyota has tendency to rear-end lightness, at present I have compensated for this by sticking two hundredweight millet-sacks in boot, but this is only stop-gap measure since what you are doing is forcing weight down onto aft wishbone, this has knock-on drag effect on rear differential, plus sump banging on road, hence oil on nose, I have very likely shredded a gasket, the stuff is seeping from the bell-housing like loose bowel motion from broody pullet, next question?'

There was a long pause, punctuated by sporadic snores and the odd whimper. Several members of the audience had begun reading *Gizzard Parasite Leaflet Number 86*. In one of the darker corners, two elderly pluckers were huddled over a Mah Jong board, normally a hanging offence. At last, the Chairman himself said:

'Glorious poultry exemplar Sun Guiying, your dazzling achievement shames us all. I should like to begin tonight's dialectical proceedings by pointing the finger at myself. What have I been doing wrong?

'You have been cycling in the middle of the road,' replied Sun Guiying, 'you dozy old sod. What are you?'

'I am a dozy old sod,' muttered the Chairman.

'Do you think you own the road?'

'Yes I think I own the road.'

Sun Guiying turned from the Chairman to the audience.

'How many other cyclists here think they own the road?'

Gradually, some sixty per cent of the hall rose slowly and sheepishly to its feet.

'ALL CYCLISTS THINK THEY OWN THE ROAD!' shouted the heroine.

One by one, the rest of the audience stood up.

'ALL CYCLISTS THINK THEY OWN THE ROAD!' they shouted back, and sat down again.

'It may interest you to know,' said Sun Guiying, straightening her nylon rally-jacket and sending the highlights skating across her heavy bust, 'that it can take up to one hundred metres to stop car travelling at 100 kph *in normal conditions*, let alone eggs all over road, bloody chickens running off pavement without warning, droppings everywhere, it is like a skating rink, does anyone have any idea what I am driving on?'

An elderly lady, nudged to her feet by her front-row neighbours, stood up, hung her head, wept, banged her frail breast.

'No-one has any idea what you are driving on, triumphant egg champion hero,' she sobbed. 'Forgive us.'

'Mixed radials and cross-ply is what I am driving on!' shrieked Sun Guiying. 'Also two with canvas showing, one with pork-pellet plug, due to no bloody stocks up distributor, car is damned death-trap, got no toe-in, got no downline tracking, and suddenly road full of cycling nerds wandering all over shop, have you ever costed out wingdent repair, beat out, rub down, apply four coats metallic to match in, replace chrome trim, mastic metal-to-metal edge, re-underseal wheel-arch, make good?'

'No!' cried the old lady, and ran from the hall, scattering feathers, to hurl herself into a freezing slipper-bath, shave her head, and begin her fast.

The Chairman watched her go.

'Are we to get rid of the bicycles, incredible eggproducing paragon?' he murmured.

'And the eggs.' said Sun Guiying.

'AND THE *EGGS*?' howled the audience.

'No question,' replied Sun Guiying.

The Chairman bit his knuckle. One did not incautiously oppose a Heroine Of The Peasant Elite, an Idol Of The

Glorious Press, a Mega-Egg Producer upon whom the great sun of the Central Committee had specifically directed a major beam. He cleared his throat.

'And what, then, shall we produce?' he murmured.

'Droppings,' answered Sun Guiying.

'Chicken droppings?' croaked the Chairman.

'Are there any other kind?' said Sun Guiying. 'We shall sterilise the chickens and put them on a laxative diet, and from the droppings we shall manufacture methane, and on the methane we shall run the car. That is the way of the future! That is what progress is all about!'

The Chairman sank to his chair again, and dropped his head in his hands.

'You cannot have poached droppings on toast,' he muttered.

Sun Guiying looked at him and the audience looked at her; the dialectic had reached, surely, an insuperable crux? The heroine, however, merely smiled, strangely; and when she spoke, her voice was throaty, quivering, full of dreams.

'True,' she said.'But then again, you cannot go round Silverstone on an egg.'

Like a Tea Tray in the Sky

A gigantic planet which only just failed to become a star has been discovered at a distance of 28 light-years from the sun.   Daily Telegraph

THREE IN the midsummer morning, a sprat-coloured dawn beginning to rim the back fence, the first blackbird honking its gullet free of wormshards prior to stepping into the contralto section, and I, sleepless, tread the lawn on dew-chilled feet, smoke, and look at the duck.

It was big, but otherwise not much of a duck. It was brown, with a wall-eye, and there was an asymmetry about the beak which bespoke nonentity.

It looked back at me, from its good eye.

'Can't sleep?' said the duck.

I dropped my cigarette. It hissed in the dew, and died.

'You're a duck,' I said. You will say that emergencies find me wanting, but you had to be there.

'Inside,' said the duck, 'I'm a swan.'

'Ah,' I said.

'Look,' said the duck, 'gimme a break. The light is bad: think of me as a small swan.'

'I'll try,' I said. I lit another cigarette. It took some time.

'I don't always come down as a small swan,' said the duck. 'Sometimes I materialise in a shower of tin.'

I caught an inkling of his drift.

'Or a bull?' I suggested.

The duck looked away.

'Bull*ock*,' it muttered, as only ducks can.

'I see,' I said. 'I'm sorry.'

'I did not realise until it was too late,' continued the duck, staring fixedly at a moribund azalea. 'I came down, the plan was to mate with something really major, a waterfall, a cliff, a big oak, only when it got to the point, there was bugger-all on the end, except the -ock.'

'Tough,' I said.

'I ended up holding hands with a phonebooth,' said the duck, bitterly. 'Can you imagine the embarrassment?'

'Not entirely,' I said.

'It is not easy to be a planet,' said the duck, 'and unable to cut the mustard. You would not credit the derision, up Olympus.'

'When you are not a duck,' I said, 'which—'

'Small swan.'

'When you are not a small swan, which planet are you?'

The duck cleared its throat.

'I am the planet Dermot,' it said.

'Dermot,' I said. 'I see. Dermot.'

'What did you expect?' snapped the duck. 'Bloody Mars? Bloody Jupiter? This is only Cricklewood, sunshine, it is not Knightsbridge, it is not Park bloody Lane! You are very lucky to get the planet Dermot in your garden, I could've chosen Wembley, Crouch End, West Drayton, I could've had my pick.'

'I realise that,' I said, soothingly. 'It is simply that the planet Dermot is unfamiliar to me. Are you part of the solar system?'

'Definitely. More *in* it than *of* it, if you catch my drift, bloody snobbery being what it is, but I am a solar system planet, no question, there I am, only twenty-eight light-years from the sun, practically a stone's throw, inter-galactically speaking.'

'It seems rather far,' I said, 'to be considered the solar system.'

'Yes, it would,' said the duck, 'to a nerd. I take it you have no experience of the smarter solar suburbs?'

'None.'

'Dermot,' said the duck, 'leaves Cricklewood at the bloody post. Different class altogether. I got top-notch people walking all over me, when I'm not a duck.'

'People?'

'All right, things. But things with good accents, designer clothes, breeding, all that. There's a thing rules Dermot, she'd see your Queen off pretty bloody quick, I can tell you. She's been on the throne twelve million years, apart from anything else. What she doesn't know about ruling you could stick in your eye.'

Dawn had begun to take hold. In the east, the sun started to rise over Harrow.

'Stone me!' cried the duck, suddenly, 'What's that?'

'It's the sun,' I said.

'Get off!' exclaimed the duck. 'That's never the sun.

Look at the size of it!'

'It would, of course, be smaller on Dermot?'

'Like a walnut,' muttered the duck, morosely. 'You don't half have to wrap up warm. It's hardly surprising the things don't go out much. Dermot's dead at weekends.'

'Which is no doubt why you come to Earth so regularly?' I offered.

'Wrong,' said the duck. 'I come here because I am a god. I got responsibilities.'

'Ah, yes,' I said, nodding. 'I recall you mentioned Olympus. I assume you're on it.'

'*Near* it,' replied the duck. 'The other eight grabbed the best places, didn't they? Personally, I blame the Greeks, it is all down to them, if Archimedes had invented the telescope instead of mucking about with the bloody screw and displacement and I don't know what, I could've been discovered ages ago. I should've been up there with Neptune and Venus and Mercury and all the rest of the nobs, instead of stuck on a Peloponnesian bloody foothill with a takeaway moussaka stand and a bouzouki disco full of bloody Germans breaking plates all hours of the bloody night!'

'Never mind, Dermot,' I said, 'I'm sure you do an absolutely marvellous job as a god, whatever the premises. Which is your, er, speciality?'

'Come again?' said the duck.

'Oh, you know, war, love, the hunt, the weather, that kind of thing. What exactly are you the god *of*?'

The duck looked back at the dead azalea.

'I am the god of crockery,' it murmured.

'Crockery?'

'Plates, cups, jugs, bowls, the occasional tureen,' said the duck, 'you name it, I watch over it.'

I lit another cigarette. It had to be said.

'Given the number of breakages,' I began, as kindly as I could, 'you would not appear, if I may say so, to be doing a particularly good—'

'I cannot be bloody everywhere!' cried the duck, with such force that a crowd of breakfasting starlings burst and scattered. 'Have you any idea what crockery is like, compared with war or weather or any of the plum jobs *they* got while I was hanging about twenty-eight light years away waiting to be offered something? A god like Mars, he can get up of a morning, say *Right, I think I'll send Hitler into Poland,* and go back to bed for six years. Have you the remotest idea how many plates there are in the Universe, on top of which I am required to be a planet responsible for six billion things going on and on about the cold, plus coming down here all the time in some rotten cut-price metamorphosis nobody else'll touch? Last week, I materialised as a 1962 Cortina, I was full of rust, I had two flat tyres, and they still insisted I mate with something.'

'Any luck?'

'I had a go at a woman on a pushbike, but she got a flyer at the lights and she was up Edgware Road before I could get into second. Week before that, I came down as an artichoke. They seem to have no idea of contemporary sexual trends, up Olympus, I have not had a tumble since 1326.'

'Really?'

'I materialised as a stoat, but someone must have seen us at it. When I went back next night to found a race of minoweasels, they'd burned her at the stake.'

The sun came up into the long subsequent silence. At last, since I could think of nothing more comforting, I said:

'Look, I know a few people in Fleet Street. If it's any help, I think I could get a few words about you into the *Telegraph.*'

The duck's beak dropped. A teardrop welled in its little eye.

'You'd do that for *me?*' it said, broken-voiced.

'Why not?' I said.

The tear ran down the beak, hovered, and fell.

'How can I ever repay you?' said the duck.

'As a matter of fact,' I replied, 'I have this rather nice Chelsea tea-pot. It has a cracked spout, and a—'

'Say no more!' cried the duck.

I smiled, and thanked it, and half-bowed, as one does to a god, and turned, and walked slowly back to the house. I was almost at the door when I felt a tug at my dressing-gown hem. I looked down. The beak detached itself. 'About this teapot,' said the duck. 'Do you want it repaired, or do you want it pregnant?'

Love On The Tiller

The romantic novelist Barbara Cartland is writing a new book on Lord Mountbatten, to counter what she sees as unfair attacks on him in the recent biography by Philip Ziegler.
                               Guardian

'HEAVENS!' TRILLED Edwina Ashley, excitedly snapping her cocktail straw so that the teeny-weeny droplets of gin danced and glinted in the chandelier's costly beams like fireflies, 'I doubt that I have ever set eyes upon *anyone* so strapping!'

Hers was a wondrous combination: the lithe figure of a prominent Conservative MP's daughter, the sharp clever eyes of a Jewish quadroon, the long sensible feet of a major debutante. Small wonder that all Mayfair was at those feet, or that those eyes were immovably fixed, in their turn, upon the stern Baltic profile of the immensely tall young sailor currently swopping poop anecdotes with a rapt Noel Coward.

'How ripping,' cried the lissome Diana Duff Cooper fervently, 'to be so strapping!'

She clapped her slim hands ecstatically, so that the famous emeralds hurled back the light like little green cricketers. The tiny nose turned towards Edwina.

'Would you care to meet him?' she murmured.

Flutter, went blushing Edwina's young heart! Leap, leap, went the beads upon her presentable bosom! As if in echo, the coon band sent their heady animal rhythms thumping across the ballroom, their saucer-eyed faces shining and their huge gleaming grins seeming to cry YES! YES!

And yet, what of her own bee-sting mouth?

It opened, but nothing emerged!

She could not speak! Her lips were rooted to the spot!

For he, impossibly, wondrously, miraculously, was striding towards her—did she imagine it, or was the entire room shaking at the magisterial clump of his huge shoes?

'I say,' he said at last, through teeth white as a row of Rennies, 'do you know your mouth's wide open?'

The boldness of his wit confounded her. She dropped her dark lashes. Thankfully, Diana hurtled to the rescue.

'I say,' she cried, 'haven't we met?'

'Possibly,' he murmured, his voice like thick cocoa. 'Isn't your husband Duff?'

'Yes,' she replied, 'isn't he? Would you like to drive me home? We could blindfold the borzoi and tango till dawn!'

He smiled a fetchingly rueful smile; then, with that graceful expertise which betokens a hundred generations of breeding, simultaneously bit his lower lip, choked back a manly sob, and blinked away a brimming tear.

'I am afraid I am promised to another,' he said.

Astonishingly, this shock brought Edwina Ashley to her fugitive senses. She knew that something had to be done, and done jolly quickly!

'Has she got £2.3 million?' she cried.

Slowly, his huge liquid eyes seemed to glaze: then, very gradually, gently, they turned, swam powerfully towards her own, paused for one breathtaking instant, and dropped—but innocently—to her chic little seed-pearled frock.

'I say,' he breathed, softly, 'what an absolutely ripping bodice . . .'

. . . utterly faithful.

And yet, in the wicked, waspish, wayward world that was foolish, feckless, flapper London, the very impeccability of their behaviour acted as a red rag to a horse. Eager to besmirch the spotless reputations of the radiant newly-wed, evil lower-class people put the foulest constructions upon their most innocent activities.

On one occasion, Edwina had slipped away, as was her frequent wont, for a quiet session of rubber bridge with the rhythm section of Sambo's Struttin' Memphis Fools in their suite at the Savoy.

As she later passed through the glittering foyer, into whom should she bump but the exquisite Lady Annabel Fitzalan-Redesdale von Hesse?

'How did you get on?' enquired this *ravissante* worthy.

'I made four spades!' was the joyous reply.

Hardly had they finished their tinkling giggles, as gels will, than some dreadful squat parvenu had passed on his misconstrued eavesdropping to the jackals of the Press. They, in their vile turn, telephoned brave Louis, just back from the punishing public duty of judging a Theda Bara Lookalike Contest in the bosun's mess of *H.M.S. Chubby*.

His immeasurably witty reply was curt, quick, frosty, and so appropriately naval that I should not for one tiny moment even dream of passing on to my dear readers something best reserved for those very special moments when port is passed, cigars are lit, and gentler creatures are quite properly neither seen nor heard . . .

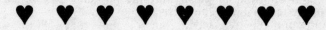

. . . with one bound he was free!

The rippling muscles flailed the icy ocean, the strong, brown, spadelike hands cleft the mighty billows, frightened fish fled from the passage of his speeding trousers; while, aft of his own plucky stern, his brave vessel, the fourth that month, sank like a, like a, like a stone.

Louis, lip jutted, arms akimbo, tuned brain racing, had fought tooth and nail with every fibre of his tigrish being and all the maritime cunning of ten thousand years of seafaring blood, bone, gristly bits, and hair, but, alas, to no avail!

The brilliant evasive manoeuvre designed to thwart a mass attack from the murderously diving Stukas which *his* field-glasses alone had been astute enough to pick up well before they turned out to be a flock of gulls had caused the ship (not for the first time totally inadequate to the demands made upon her by the world's most experienced captain) to yaw horridly. This had brought her beam-on to quite the most frightful thing a sailor can ever see!

'Torpedoes, starboard bow!' thundered Louis Mount-batten.

'Driftwood, actually,' murmured his First Officer, quite erroneously, of course, but it did not matter; his captain had already barked the order that would remove *H.M.S. Nelly* from the terrible threat, back her into a dredger, swing her against the dock, and put her at the bottom of Portsmouth harbour, safe from Nazi harm!

Only then, as he paddled courageously ashore, did he have his first thought for his own welfare, and send yet another of his famous telegrams to the Admiralty:

'HAVE BEEN SUNK DUE TO BUOYS IN ALL THE WRONG PLACES'

Which received the equally famous reply:

'HAVEN'T WE ALL, DEAR . . .'

. . . more heartrendingly pitiable than the sight of the might of Imperial Japan shuffling brokenly past in the inevitable submission to defeat.

Yellow they were, true, but somehow that yellowness had become less disgusting than an Englishman would normally think it. Failure had made it greyer; almost, well, human. Foolishly, fumblingly, feebly, they filed past, generals and bootboys, admirals and signalmen, pilots and cooks, down the steps of the elegant Singapore house into which they had so much more jauntily filed scant hours before.

They had gone in with a gleam on their boots and a glint on their ancestral swords, their spurs a-jingle and their epaulettes a-dangle, so bravely holding their slant-eyed little heads in one last game stab at dignity, as if to say *Victors we may be not, now, yet vanquished we shall never become!*

How wrong these interestingly bandy sons of the Emperor turned out to be! Within that august colonial pile, testament to a far nobler Empire than theirs could ever aspire to be, the frightful truth had at last been borne home to them. Their heads hung low, their eyes gleamed red, their tongues lolled out; some now wore one boot only, the uniforms of others hung in tatters, and many a once-jaunty jodhpur was held up not by its vanished Sam Brownn but merely by the wearer's trembling hand.

Louis, magnificent in spotless white, a dozen ribbons on his broad breast catching the bright September sun, stood, brow furrowed, in the drive, and, as they slouched from the great mansion, raised his hand in one final, formal salute.

Last down the steps, fresh as a fuchsia, tripped the ravishing Edwina, deftly restoring to her lovely lips the gleaming carmine which no lady *d'un certain age* must ever be without.

Her handsome husband turned.

'What's up, Woozle?' he enquired, tenderly.

'The Nips have just surrendered, Uncle Wonky,' she replied.

The fine Battenburg forehead became yet wrinklier with bemusement, and even more swooningly attractive.

'I rather think, dearest Pongle,' he murmured, 'that they were supposed to do it to *me*.'

'Oh surely not!' cried Edwina, her high, gay, silvery laugh ringing down the colonnaded poplars like a tinkling temple bell and startling the . . .

. . . describe the India which, upon that fateful day in 1947, greeted the eyes, ears, and noses of the world's most glamorous and devoted couple? A thousand peculiar smells and millions and millions of little brown wrinkled beings in old sheets running about and shouting 'By Jove!' at one another is probably as sure a way as any of summing up that seething, teeming, broiling sub-continent poised to embark on quite the silliest escapade of its history.

That the heat was quite intolerable *va sans dire*. Even Edwina had begun to glow a little, and as for the servants, it was well-nigh impossible to stop their incomprehensible gabbling long enough to explain, in her fluent sign-language, the necessity for regular use of Pink Camay on all hidden surfaces, especially where a tricky crevice was involved.

Imagine, therefore, her joy when a little nut-brown fellow turned up at her door who seemed to have a basic grasp of English and to change his funny little tubular long johns reasonably regularly! He it was who—since Louis was often away for days on end doing the very very important things that viceroys have to do—gradually managed to initiate the puzzled Edwina in all the mystic ways of his peculiar tribe, from how to avoid ruining a perfectly good mosquito net by not throwing your arms and legs about too much, to conserving that precious commodity, water, by rejecting the basic selfishness of taking one's bath alone.

Teacher, friend, man-about-the-house, cook (it was just for her that he created his Edwina Curry, that dish which has brought the strongest stomach to its knees), Pandit Nehru, within a few short months, had soon made himself utterly indispensable to the Mistress, as she was of course known to all who loved and . . .

The Gospel According to St Durham

... and Jesus went forth, and saw a great multitude, and was moved by compassion toward them, and he healed the sick with the blue mould that he had scraped off the five loaves that he had brought.

15 And when it was evening, his disciples came to him, saying, Shut the surgery, none of these people has an appointment anyhow, send them away that they may go into the villages and buy themselves some victuals.

16 But Jesus said unto them, They need not depart; give ye them to eat.

17 And they said unto him, We have here but two loaves and five fishes.

18 And Jesus said, It is *five* loaves and *two* fishes, for the umpteenth time, why does everyone always get that wrong, two loaves and five fishes would be tricky, but five loaves and two fishes is a doddle, we could even cut off the crusts.

19 And he took the two fishes, and he hung them over the fire a little while.

20 And his disciples marvelled, saying, What is this miracle that thou art performing now?

21 And he said unto them, It is called smoked salmon, you slice it very thin and you put it on titchy pieces of bread, you would not credit the number of people you can cater for, it will change the face of bar mitzvahs as we know them.

22 And lo! The miracle of the canapé was done, and the disciples went around with twelve trays, and the multitude said, Terrific, but what about the little slices of lemon?

23 And Jesus said unto them, Look up into the trees, and the people were amazed, for they had never realised that the things in the trees were lemons, they had only ever seen lemons in slices at catered functions.

24 And they that had eaten were about five thousand men, beside women and children and gatecrashers who had pretended to be distant relatives on the bride's side.

25 And straightaway Jesus constrained his disciples to get into a ship, and to go before him unto the other side, while he sent the multitudes away, and he went up into a mountain apart to pray.

26 But the ship was now in the midst of the sea, tossed with waves; for the wind was contrary.

27 And in the fourth watch of the night Jesus went unto them, walking on the sea.

28 And when the disciples saw him, they were troubled, saying, It is a spirit; and they cried out for fear.

29 But straightway Jesus spake unto them, saying, Be of good cheer; it is I and this is the breast-stroke, be not afraid.

30 And Peter answered him and said, Lord, if it be thou, bid me come unto thee on the water.

31 And Jesus said, You do your legs like a frog and you push with your hands, but the main thing is not to panic.

32 And Peter was come down out of the ship, and walked on the water, to go to Jesus. But when he saw the wind boisterous, he was afraid; and beginning to sink, he cried, saying, Lord save me.

33 And immediately Jesus stretched forth his hand and caught him, and said unto him, O thou of little faith, if thou hadst merely turned upon thy back and not panicked, thou wouldst have floated, it is simple hydrodynamics, one day all Jews will swim, personally I blame Moses, parting the Red Sea was just mollycoddling people.

34 And the disciples gazed upward, fearing that the clouds would part and a great finger would come down and poke their boat, because the Red Sea plan had been God's idea in the first place.

35 But that did not happen; instead, the wind ceased, probably because God had conceded the point. And they that were in the ship came and worshipped Jesus, saying, Of a truth thou art the Son of God.

14 AND after the miracle of the smoked salmon, Jesus was much in demand at big affairs.

2 And the third day thereafter, there was a marriage in Cana of Galilee; and the mother of Jesus was there.

3 And both Jesus was called, and his disciples, to the marriage. And the disciples murmured amongst them-

selves, saying, Wonder what it'll be this time, five cocktail sticks and two little sausages? The miracle of the croquette potato?

4 But it was the wine, this time, and when they wanted wine, the mother of Jesus said unto him, They have no wine.

5 Jesus said unto her, Woman, what have I to do with thee? Mine hour is not yet come.

6 But his mother replied in this wise, saying, Who is talking about hours being come, this is no big deal, this is just one of your smart tricks with the wine, so that I am not ashamed of the son that I have borne, his catering is already a household word all over.

7 And Jesus said, Trick?

8 And his mother said, All right, miracle. And she said unto the servants, Whatsoever he saith unto you, do it.

9 And there were set there six water-pots of stone, after the manner of the purifying of the Jews, containing two or three firkins apiece.

10 Jesus said unto the servants, Fill the water-pots with water. And they filled them up to the brim.

11 And he turned to his disciples and he said, What kind of people throw a big funtion but do not lay on wine?

12 And Simon Peter said, How about people who never drink wine, Lord?

13 And Jesus said, Right in one, verily are there no flies on thee, Simon Peter, brother of Andrew. Thus shall the water be drawn from these water-pots and we shall pass among the guests with the cups, saying in this wise, It is a naive domestic Burgundy without any breeding, but I think you'll be amused by its presumption.

14 And he said unto the servants, Draw out now, and bear unto the governor of the feast. And they bore it.

15 And his disciples moved among the multitude, and very soon vast numbers in that multitude were saying, No more for me, it goeth straight to my head, and Good colour, lasts well, a plucky little wine, if a trifle farmyard, and Perhaps not quite forward enough yet, but well worth laying down a case or two.

15 AFTER this there was a feast of the Jews: and Jesus went up to Jerusalem.

2 Now there is at Jerusalem by the sheep *market* a pool, which is called in the Hebrew tongue Bethesda, having five porches.

3 And a certain man was there, which had an infirmity, waiting for the waters of the pool to be moved by an angel so that he might step in and be made whole.

4 Because that was the kind of crackpot superstition Jesus had to put up with all his working life.

5 When Jesus saw the man lie, and knew that he had been a long time *in that case,* he said unto him, Wilt thou be made whole?

6 Because Jesus had been around, and he had learned a thing or two about psychosomasis; and he knew that *wilt* was half the battle.

7 And the man answered him, Sir, I was at this wedding at Cana a few days back, and they had this really good stuff there, I must have put away a firkin and I have this mother and father of all hangovers, my legs are like unto rubber, plus shooting pains all over.

8 And Simon Peter said unto Jesus, You were not wrong about the psychosomatic stuff, Lord. Wilt thou tell him, or shall I?

9 And Jesus said, You are only my registrar, this is a job for the consultant.

10 And straightaway he told the man about the water at Cana.

11 And the man said unto him Art thou serious?

12 Jesus said unto him, Rise, take up thy bed, and walk.

13 And immediately the man was made whole, and took up his bed, and walked: and on the same day was the Sabbath.

14 Therefore the Jews said unto him that was cured, It is the sabbath day: it is not lawful for thee to carry thy *bed.*

15 He answered them, He that made me whole, the same said unto me, Take up thy bed, and walk.

16 Then asked they him, What man is that which said unto thee take up thy bed and walk on the Sabbath?

17 And he answered them, saying: A doctor.

18 And the Jews said, A qualified man? That's different.

Nuclear Spring

Nordic agriculturalists have set up the world's first gene bank at Spitzbergen, where they are saving the seeds of 50,000 plants. In the event of a nuclear war, survivors would be able to find all the necessary seeds to start growing crops again. Daily Telegraph

CHAIRMAN: Good evening, and welcome to *Gardeners' Question Time* from the village hall here at Charnel Magna, jewel of the Snowdonia plain, where I'm sure the large audience has a veritable host of fascinating questions to put to our panel of experts! So without further ado, let's plunge straight in and take a question from the small monocular gentleman holding his breast up in the front row, Mr Bagley, is it?

BAGLEY: Yes, mainly. One leg is Harris. My question is about rhododendrons. I have normally got a good crop of fruit off of them, but this year they are small and wrinkly and when I try to pick them, they bite. Look at this thumb, it is hardly more than a stump. I have tried gathering windfalls, but as soon as I make a move, they run away. I am not as spry as I used to be, and Harris has got a funny knee. Do the experts have any suggestions to make?

CHAIRMAN: Thank you, Mr Bagley, an interesting point. One, I think, for you, Arthur?

ARTHUR: Yes, indeed, unless I am very much mistaken this is our old friend, *parturient montes*. Under certain circumstances—a volcanic April, say, a sudden unseasonal hole in the Heavyside Layer, a gust or two of khaki wind, too much strontium in the mulch—rhododendrons can occasionally bear mice. They are not, of course, normal domestic mice—few of them, for example, have more than three eyes, and their webs are extremely sticky—but mice they are, nevertheless.

BAGLEY: What is their jam like?

ARTHUR: It differs slightly from ordinary rhododendron jam in that it has bones in it. It also has a somewhat gamey flavour, but is really quite pleasant, especially as a poultice. As Harris is not up to running about, your best course would be to gas the tree first and then knock the ripe mice off with a rake.

CHAIRMAN: Thank you, Arthur. I think the person on either side of Mr Bagley has a question, now? The Misses Rhoda and Valerie Skeat, I believe?

THE MISSES SKEAT: Yes, thank you. We have been joined at the left fingertips since birth, and, not to put too fine a point on it, we find topiary something of a problem. Our garden is surrounded by a mango hedge which for the past eight years we have been trying to shape into a series of peacocks holding one another's trunks, but it grows faster than we are able to snip it. It does not look like peacocks, it looks like sod-all, and we are afraid of becoming a laughing-stock. The problem is we each have a right hand on one handle of the shears, and it is impossible to co-ordinate the cutting, never mind losing the odd nose, three off already since Easter, and then there's the—

CHAIRMAN: Let me stop you there, ladies. Your question, I take it, concerns the availability of Siamese shears?

THE MISSES SKEAT: No, our question concerns is there anything easier than peacocks? Can the panel recommend a book of simple hedge-shapes for the, er, hard-of-shearing?

CHAIRMAN: A tricky one, Denzil?

DENZIL: Not really. Something of an old chestnut, in fact. Whatever that is. I get asked this question a lot, especially in the swampier counties, where a hedge is very often the only thing that grows. The best book I know is Lord Lucan's *Green Lumps,* which starts off with rudimentary cubes such as frogs and bananas, and goes on to really complicated things like an Elizabethan maze hewn out of privet fly-traps.

CHAIRMAN: Goodness me, Denzil, that sounds a tricky proposition!

DENZIL: You wouldn't chuckle, Chairman. If you don't find your way out inside ten minutes, it'll have your arm off.

CHAIRMAN: Any comments of a botanical nature, Dr Greenslade?

DR GREENSLADE: Arf! Arf!

DENZIL: I don't know why we bring him, he hasn't published anything since he was a puppy.

CHAIRMAN: Well, then, let's get on, I believe someone has a

question about greenfly, a Mr Foskett, if I can, ha ha, read my writing, I must have written it with my sock on, *is* it Mr Foskett?

FOSKETT: That is correct. I am a keen rose-grower, and this year I have found the greenfly almost more than I can stand. They keep pulling up my Ena Harknesses, banging on the front door, and yelling ROSES, ROSES, CALL THESE BLOODY ROSES, THERE'S NOT ENOUGH ON THESE TO FEED A HORSE! I wouldn't care, but we pass all our old clothes on to them, and we've had 'em in for Christmas for the past eight years, I am at my wit's end to know what to do for the best.

CHAIRMAN: Arthur, you're the greenfly expert, I believe?

ARTHUR: I wouldn't say expert, but, yes, I've learned a bit about their ways over the years, they *can* be pests around the garden, and they do seem to be particularly large this year, I think all that fatty brown rain in, when was it, October, probably has something to do with it, that and the muck from the Wembley glacier, but I've found you can reach a modus vivendi with them if you're prepared to give and take a bit, lend them the car now and then, that kind of thing. At least they're better than bloody blackfly, parties all night, banging dustbin lids, doing it in daylight on the lawn—

CHAIRMAN: Steady, Arthur. Some blackfly can be extremely—

ARTHUR: I speak as I find, Chairman. I may be just an ordinary English country bloke, I may not be an educated Airedale like Dr Greenslade here, I may not have your three heads or Denzil's gift for hanging by his tail, but when it comes to blackfly, I think the majority of the audience in this hall would see eye to—

FOSKETT: Never mind blackfly, what about the big green bastards kicking my dry-stone walls down?

CHAIRMAN: Sorry, Mr Foskett, the experts did get side-tracked there! Denzil, perhaps you've got the answer to Mr Foskett's pest problem?

DENZIL: Well, Chairman, perhaps I have. In a word, Mr Foskett—*ladybirds*. The old remedies are still the best. Your average ladybird will eat five thousand greenfly in a day, you know.

FOSKETT: Ladybird, ladybird, where would I keep a ladybird? I've only got four acres, give or take, you wouldn't get a long enough runway in even if you was to lay it diagonal, don't even talk about the droppings. If it's a question of ladybirds, I'd rather pull the roses up and plant asparagus, they may pong a bit but they make a nice fur coat, I'd rather be warm of a winter than have to sit there watching a twelve-ton marsupial with big black spots blowing the thatch off every time it comes in to land, thank you very much!

DR GREENSLADE: Arf! Arf!

DENZIL: For God's sake, somebody give him a biscuit!

CHAIRMAN: Yes, listeners, once again my impatient colleague Dr Greenslade gnawing on my trusty old dandelion stick means it's time for all of us to go walkies, I'm afraid! We've rather left poor Mr Foskett hanging, haven't we, so if anybody wishes to drop him a line, and that of course goes for any of you greenfly who may be listening, don't hesitate to post your suggestions to Broadcasting Hole. Next week, we'll be crossing the Cotswold Desert to meet a fascinating group of Oxford bedouin who claim to have succeeded in growing goats from tubers to produce a cheese-bearing dahlia able to march in front of a regimental band. It promises to be a riveting programme, so if you're in the neighbourhood, look out for us then. I'm the three-headed one, and I'll be riding on Arthur, as usual, with dear old prehensile Denzil hanging from my left arm and Dr Greenslade dragging along behind. And as I always say, he's lucky he's still got a long behind to drag! Cheerio!

Yellow Perils

WHO WOULD have thought, a little month ago, that I, wet but conservative, woolly but liberal, fan of Dorset scents and Wiltshire sausages, hardback buyer, anti-centrist, BUPA member, lover of Gold Flake and *Adlestrop* and the original AA badge, gourmet, mortgagee, defender of three-piece suits, ballroom dancing medalholder (bronze, 1954), supporter of free trade unions and private education, monogamist, occasional Sotheby's underbidder, claret-layer, gardener, leather-brogue-wearer, unsliced bread advocate, owner of a lever-action watch and a Swan fountain pen, Metrolander, beef-buff—who would have thought that I of all traditionalists should be sitting here alone in the summer gloaming and weeping over the erosion of Chinese communism?

Not that I ever actively supported it. The transmogrification of a myriadfold culture into one billion asexual cyclist in fog-hued pyjamas always had its dispiriting side, and when they subsequently took to both formation-swimming in hats and enriching plutonium, the concerned Westerner could not but feel that the ideogram was on the wall and that it was only a matter of time before they were all standing on the Isle of Wight with rice on their boots, endorsing not-unnatural suspicions that we were about to have a nasty occident.

It did not, however, happen.

What happened, if I may plead exigencies of space in so abbreviating the current sinological overview, is that Mao handed in his lunchbucket, various people with chiming names were hung out to dry, and before we knew it, raffish dark blue uniforms were appearing sporadically among the grey, to be rapidly followed by imported Polish lace-ups counterpointing the rope espadrilles, a few old Beatles LPs, bound numbers of *The Tatler & Bystander* on open sale in downtown Beijing, and, as reported recently in these pages, the first privately owned peasant motor-car. Thus, the profit-motive—springing, like the Western hope it engendered, eternal in the human breast—seemed to spell the end of inscrutable totalitarianism, and the advent of the mellow yellow.

It would, of course, come about very, very slowly.

The Chinese had, after all, spent a generation-and-a-half in literal self-abnegation: go out of a morning with check socks or an unlicensed sideburn, and the Red Guards would have had you before you reached the bikepound. Strap your watch onto your right wrist, and you were looking at six months in a tin trunk with communal criticism coming through the slot twenty-four hours a day. Laugh in the wrong place during *The Triumph of Magneto Operative Wang Over The Poisonous Revisionist Conspiracy Engendered By Deviant Running-Dog Axle Inspector Ho,* and you would still be dangling from the dress circle by your thumbs when the show went into its third chart-topping year.

Liberation has to be introduced into such thorough indoctrination a drop at a time, like oil into incipient mayonnaise. In 1985, I had imagined, they would allow the plain necktie; stripes would not arrive until 1990. It would be well into the twenty-first century before the authorities sanctioned the windsor knot. The spotted bow could take an eon.

Because the Chinese administration was resistant to exploitation. Exploitation was the vilest pictogram in the deck. Torremolinos may have turned overnight from a fishing village into a deep-fried Luton, Corfu may have become Stuttgart-am-See, but that was because they wanted to be. Greed was their credo, and China's anathema.

Plus, all ideological considerations apart, there was the sheer size of the place. The street-wise sophisticate in Shanghai could probably come to terms with, say, the zip-fly, given half an hour and the owner's manual, but three thousand miles away, beyond the Hwang-Ho, there are Mongolian sheperds tending their woks by night to whom the humble button is an arcane mystery fraught with superstition and terror.

I liked the idea of capitalist gradualism. It seemed to me to be the hope not only of China, but of the world, and, even more cheeringly, of Britain. The world, which had begun to go wrong at the point at which Cain wanted to be better off than Abel without putting in the hours, could be remade, very slowly.

Of all the Western industrial nations, Britain would best be suited by that particular mood. We can make things only very slowly, which would ideally have complemented the Chinese policy of introducing things very slowly. British engineers, technologists, builders, planners, manufacturers would have gone out to China, probably by ship, and passed quiet Sino-British decades working things out and doing them.

We should thus, jointly, have constructed winding roads, without clover-leaves, and elliptical roundabouts with geraniums on them. We should have built inchoate little towns, unribboned developments of cob cottages with exposed and probably wormy beams, and buckled walls, and thatched roofs, full of birds' nests, so that the delighted owners would never be short either of charm or of soup. We should have interspersed these with village greens whose duckponds would, like the roofs, provide both rural colour and crispy sustenance, and we should have encircled these greens with pubs that served *real* real ale in pewter mugs, while back in Copenhagen and Ulm lager-brewers would be slitting their throats at the failure of hard-sell techniques that had elsewhere made flatulence a market-leader.

British tailors would have—gradually, calmly—introduced the plus-four and the checked cap, after long years of unfair desuetude, and our motor-manufacturers would (despite *British Leyland* being a shibboleth from which the Chinese lip will ever shy) set up regional plants where Lanchesters and Armstrong-Siddeleys and Crossleys and Frazer-Nashes would be hand-built by cunning Chinese craftsmen under the benevolent supervision of spotlessly white-coated British foremen, all of whom would look like Bernard Lee.

They would have leather suitcases in the boot.

Which they would drive to airports we should have built for them, with red-brick control towers and windsocks, but they would not be called airports, they would be called aerodromes, and they would have basketwork armchairs in them, and Chinese trios in three-piece dinner-suits would play Ivor Novello medleys while the travellers sipped gimlets and sidecars and waited for the stewards to finish putting freesias in the cabin vases of the Handley-Page so that it could be cleared for take-off.

We should have. . .

But why go on? What point in torturing oneself with dreams of the might-have-been reconstruction of a writ-large profitable English idyll, ten million square miles of the undeveloped world ripe for translation into a paradise of pre-lapsarian taste and now made over in the image of Haslemere?

The bloody Frogs have beaten us to it.

'Following hard upon the successful opening of Maxim's in Beijing, the introduction of Pernod to the Chinese people, and the setting-up of the Pierre Cardin clothing operation,' the *Financial Times* this morning tells me, 'China yesterday signed a sixty-million-franc deal to set up its first *Club Méditerranée* holiday village.'

Since you have hurled this book aside, screamed, kicked the cat, and snatched the book up again to discover whether your eyes have deceived you, you have had, I take it, plenty of time for the full horror to sink in: a thousand million souls in navy-blue designer vests and lemon perma-prest slacks and those appalling white basketwork shoes, reeking of unisex aerosol musk as they jolt from one vast bogus holiday kraal to another in fifty million Mao-grey *deux chevaux* like tin woodlice, there to strip themselves naked for shrieking volleyball, shrieking barbecues, shrieking windsurfing, shrieking pétanque, shrieking copulation, and shrieking al fresco discomania to the strains, quite literally, of Johnny 'Alliday's antique glottis, while simultaneously boozing themselves legless on imported tankerloads of glaucous gunk which gives off a pollutant pong that, in any civilised country, attracts only beagles.

And, worst of all, no place for me.

It would have been pleasant to have seen out my days in the shadow of The Old Vicalage, Glantchester, teaching the village blacksmith how to deal with a short rising ball outside the off stump, but it's too late, now.

Yesterday in Parliament

HOUSE OF COMMONS
OFFICIAL REPORT

PARLIAMENTARY DEBATES
(HANSARD)

The House met at half-past Two o'clock
PRAYERS
(Mr. SPEAKER *in the Chair*)
ORAL ANSWERS TO QUESTIONS
EUROPEAN COMMUNITY
Switzerland

Mr. Elwin Croft asked the Secretary of State for Foreign and Commonwealth Affairs what plans he has to visit Basel.

The Secretary of State for Foreign and Commonwealth Affairs (Sir Geoffrey Howe): None, sir.

Mr. Croft: In advance of his plans to visit Basel, will the right hon. Gentleman tell the House the attitude of Her Majesty's Government to Switzerland becoming a member of the European Community?

Sir Geoffrey Howe: Any application which might be made by the Swiss Government would be to the Community as a whole, and Her Majesty's Government would be only one of the members to take a view of it. But, clearly, Her Majesty's Government's attitude could not but reflect our warm affection for Britain's oldest ally. Could anything ever erase the memory of those dark days when we two stood shoulder to shoulder and alone against the dark shadow of whatever it was that was threatening civilisation as we knew it?

Hon. Members:Hear! Hear! Plucky little Switzerland! Ils ne passeront pas! Remember the Alamo! etc.

Mr. Winston Churchill: Gentlemen, I recall the words of my illustrious grandfather—

Mr. Clement Freud: Wasn't he an Austrian psychologist?

Mr. Churchill: The hon. Member of Ely may well be right, but I cannot for the life of me see why that fact should prevent me from recalling his words. As he so succinctly—

Mr. Croft: Be that as it may, and hon. Members must not think me uncognizant of the unique role which that proud country played in standing firm when the storm clouds gathered in, er, 1928—

Hon. Members: 1934! 1946! 1898! Last Thursday! etc.

Mr. Croft: Whenever. Be that, I say, as it may, I do not think we should allow nostalgia or ancient loyalties to cloud our economic judgement. While none of us would impugn the courage of Herr Johnny Gurkha—

Hon. Member: They bought us time! Ask Chamberlain! Tell him, Neville!

Mr. Croft:—while none of us would impugn Swiss fighting grit, I say, can any of us deny that their economic reliability is somewhat less rugged?

Sir Geoffrey Howe: I trust that my hon. Friend is not going to bring up the Southport Bubble yet again?

Mr. Croft: As a matter of fact, Mr. Speaker, I was not. Do the words Ground Nut Scheme strike a familiar note?

Hon. Members: No.

Mr. Croft: Typical! If I may refresh what I take to be hon. Members' tactically poor memories (*cries of 'Oh!'*), the Ground Nut Scheme was an ill-starred attempt to restructure the Swiss tax system, thought up by William Hill.

Mr. Dennis Skinner: Rubbish! William Hill invented the postage stamp.

Hon. Members: Tripe! Cobblers!

Mr. Speaker: Order!

Mr. Skinner: He did it for a bet.

Mr. Speaker: Order! I think both hon. Gentlemen will find that they are, upon reflection, mistaken. William Hill was, as I recall, the site of the Great Exhibition of 1871, before it was burned down and moved to Lambeth Palace.

Mr. Croft: With the greatest respect, Mr. Speaker, I must insist that William Hill put a ground nut on his father's head and threw a brick at it, in a foolhardy attempt to avoid paying VAT. If further proof were needed, I would draw hon. Member's attention to the fact that Mozart wrote a famous overture about it.

Hon. Members: Name that tune!

Mr. Croft: *The Magic Brick.*

Sir Geoffrey Howe: Loath as I am to impute to my hon. Friend any intention deliberately to mislead this House, I would ask him seriously to reflect whether *The Magic Brick* to which he so confidently refers might not perhaps have been the vessel in which Sir Walter Scott circumnavigated the South Pole with Ken Livingstone and found Stanley the Gibbon?

Dr. David Owen: What?

Sir Geoffrey Howe: The beginning of evolution. They were looking for a breadfruit. Some of the greatest things in history have been accidents. Look at Gandhi. When the lid blew off the kettle, he thought he'd invented the aeroplane. Little did he realise it was the beginning of tea.

Mr. Churchill: On a point of information, was it or was it not, however, the French who invented cake?

Mr. David Penhaligon: If I may be permitted to answer the hon. Gentleman, Mr Speaker, the answer is yes. I do not wish to take up too much of the House's time on this, but cake was invented by Marie Curie, the mistress of Joe Louis. She found it growing in a little dish on the window-sill.

Sir Geoffrey Howe: At Versailles?

Mr. Penhaligon: I should need notice of that question, Mr Speaker. I have the feeling that it was Hitler at Versailles.

Mr. Speaker: On the window-sill? What was Hitler doing on the window-sill at Versailles?

Mr. Norman Fowler: He was probably going to jump.

Sir Geoffrey Howe: I don't follow.

Hon. Members: Shame! (*Laughter*)

Mr. Fowler: He was always committing suicide. He once tried to blow himself up in a briefcase. Then he married Wernher von Braun and set light to the pair of them. If you ask me, he wasn't all there. I do not believe it is stretching the credibility of this House to suggest he might have jumped out of the window at Versailles.

Mr. Croft: I am grateful to the hon. Members for their points of information, but I somehow feel we are moving away from the main thrust of the debate, which is to reassure ourselves that this great House and, even more, the great nation for which it speaks, is not plunged headlong, willy-nilly, into a political liaison we might all live to regret. I do not wish to reopen old wounds, but it is not so very long since that this island race—

Mr. Fowler: I've just remembered about Versailles. It wasn't a window-sill, it was a railway carriage. He was going to throw himself under a railway carriage.

Mr. Speaker: Order!

Mr. Croft:—this island rave found itself threatened by the greatest armada the world had yet seen!

Hon. Members: But were they Swiss?

Other Hon. Members: How do we know, what are we, walking bloody encyclopaedias, £17,702 per annum, you can't even buy *Beano,* never mind keeping up with the latest information on armadas, withdraw, yield, resign, etc.

Mr. Speaker: Order! Order! If there are any more interruptions of this kind, I warn the House that I shall have no other course but to try to find out what my predecessors would have done in my place, the office of Speaker goes back to the year dot, as I understand it, they must have the rules written down somewhere, it'll be in a big book, if I'm any judge.

Mr. Croft: I apologise if I have been the unwitting cause of any unseemliness, Mr Speaker, I wished only to draw the attention of this House to one simple truth. What was it Marx said?

Mr. Freud: He said *Either this man's dead or my watch has stopped.*

Mr. Croft: He said that those who fail to learn from the mistakes of history are doomed to repeat them. That holds true whether or not we are talking of armadas or, or, or—I don't know—helicopters.

Mr. Leon Brittan: What?

Mr. Douglas Hurd: I think he said elephants.

Mr. Peter Walker: Yes, it was definitely elephants.

Mr. George Younger: I can confirm that. He said elephants.

Mr. Norman Tebbit: Good God, yes, clear as a bell, elephants.

Mr. Nigel Lawson: Elephants, all right. No question.

The Prime Minister (Mrs. Margaret Thatcher): For the record, Mr Speaker, I should like to put it to my hon. Friend that he said elephants.

Mr. Croft: Yes, I did. I said elephants. I don't make mistakes over things of that nature.

Mrs. Thatcher: Do you know, he really is terribly, terribly good like that.

Mr. Speaker: Let the record stand.

The House rose at 5.20.

The Men from Porlock

Coleridge, in 1797, living at a lonely farmhouse on the confines of Somerset and Devon, fell asleep in his chair when reading a passage relating to the Kubla Khan and the palace that he commanded to be built. On awakening, he was conscious of having composed in his sleep two or three hundred lines on this theme, and immediately began to set down the lines that form the fragment. He was then unfortunately interrupted, and, on returning to his task, found that the remainder of the poem had passed from his memory. The Oxford Companion to English Literature

THE SUN now rose upon the right: out of the sea came he, cleared the little hill just to the east of Dunscribblin, slanted through a small and somewhat ragged copse, lanced the bedroom mullion, and hit Samuel Taylor Coleridge full in the left, lidded, eye.

It snapped open.

'Oh!' cried the poet, and shot bolt upright from the hip, like a sprung hinge. 'Dear God!'

His head seethed metrically, intricated images slotted themselves, with an audible internal click, along neat parallel lines, as if each word were a bright bead upon an abacus.

It was all there.

He slid his bony legs sideways, carefully, to clear the bed, not wanting to shake his head for fear any motion would produce a glass-paperweight effect and the words would fly up and whirl haphazardly within his dome and settle who knew where. He trod, still in his nightshirt, down the narrow staircase, over the snoring cats, into his little study, up to his cluttered escritoire, and sat gingerly down, reaching, simultaneously, for his quill.

His lips moved, tremblingly.

> *'In Xanadu did Kubla Khan*
> *A stately pleasure-dome decree:*
> *Where Sind, the sacred river, ran*
> *Through . . .'*

It was all right. It was all still there, intact. He took the quill from its inkstand, slid a piece of paper in front of him, and began to write.

He had got as far as 'Where' when something rapped on the window beside him. The quill fell from his fingers; the blot spread. His body was rigid. Excrement, thought Coleridge, and turned.

A face was staring at him through the pane, bearded, cheery, gap-toothed. Behind it, another. Both touched their mudcaked caps. Coleridge cursed again, and opened the window.

'Morning,' said the bearded man, 'squire. On the dot!'

'Dot?' said Coleridge, faintly.

'Punctuality is our watchword,' said the bearded man. 'We quote six a.m., six a.m. is what you get.'

'As per ours of the 14th ultimo,' said the man behind him. He came closer, peered in. 'Still in your nightshirt, then? All right for some! I say all right for some! I wouldn't mind his job, Alf, am I wrong? I say I wouldn't mind his job!'

Coleridge ran a thin furred tongue over his lips.

'Could you tell me what this is about?' he murmured.

'Porlock Landscaping and Garden Sundries, Lawns Laid, Ditches Dug, Trees Lopped, You Name It, At This Address Since 1762,' said Alf.

'Capabilism is our watchword,' said his colleague.

Alf produced a spattered docket, stabbed at it with a loamy forefinger.

'To sorting out existing shambles, building Dutch wall, laying turves as per deemed necessary, assembling gazebo on site, glazing same, decorating same inside and out with two coats best Jacobean green, making good, leaving site as we would wish to find it, seven pound three and eight-pence,' he read.

Coleridge slumped, expelled air, nodded slowly.

'I had forgotten,' he said. 'Could you just get on with it?'

'Say no more,' said Alf.

'Alacrism is our watchword,' said his assistant.

They went off, whistling atonally, and began dragging gazebo components off their cart. At the clatter, rooks rose, cawing, from the little copse, a far dog barked, the cats woke up on the stairs, and began fighting.

Coleridge stared at the wheeling birds. He had entirely forgotten the gazebo. It had seemed a wondrous idea at the time, it would unblock his imagination, he would sit in it, hermetically sealed within his new landscape, and write amazing stuff. That was no doubt why he had dreamed as he had dreamed—the pleasure-dome was *his,* Xanadu was *here, he* was Khan. Refreshed, he looked down at the paper, took up the pen:

'Where Alf, the sacred river, ran,' he wrote, 'Through caverns . . .'

He looked at the wet line. There was something wrong with it. He searched in his head for the original, but the essential word had gone.

After an hour, he settled for Alph. It looked marginally better.

> 'Through caverns measureless to man
> Down to a sunless sea.
> So twice five miles of fertile ground
> With turr—'

'Where's this Dutch wossname, wall, supposed to go, then?' echoed a cry across the garden, making the little Meissen figures on the study mantelpiece hop and tinkle.

'Look at the bloody plan!' shrieked Alf.

'With walls *and towers were girdled round,'* wrote Coleridge eventually, stabbing the words onto the page, breaking the quill. He read the line again, several times. I'll come back to it, he thought.

Because if he dwelt on it, he might well lose the incredible, shimmering, still-intact stanza in which each crenellation of those towers, each jalousie, each embrasure, each parados, each lunette and contravallation, each buttress and redan, each . . .

A shadow, as he dipped his resharpened quill, fell across the waiting paper.

'Run into a bit of a problem,' said Alf.

'Nothing we can't handle, probably,' said his assistant. 'Improvism is our watchword.'

'Go away,' said Coleridge, weakly. Ink dripped from his interrupted quill, onto his bare knee.

'I think you ought to take a look at it,' insisted Alf. 'We could be talking about a bob or two here.'

Slowly, the poet rose, crept back-bowed to the door, went out into the harsh sunlight; looked, staggered, fell back against the cottage wall.

106

The former lawn was a boggy mass of mud and running rivulets. As he watched, favourite shrubs sailed by and disappeared, rock-plants bobbed, briefly, and sank, an old and much-loved sundial keeled slowly over, and was swallowed up.

'Struck a main conduit,' said Alf. 'Spade went straight through, pipework was like a bloody eggshell, you should've warned us, we do not have eyes in the back of our heads, do we, Esmond?'

'It is not down to us,' said Esmond. 'Personally, I blame that japonica, you do not want to plant japonica near a mains conduit, squire, them roots shoot through 'em like bleeding rivets.'

Coleridge stared gloomily at the tree. As it began to lean, its blossom detached itself, and fluttered down in clouds.

'It appears to be dying,' he said.

'Yes,' said Alf, 'it would.'

'They do that,' said Esmond.

'I'm going inside,' said Coleridge. 'Do what you can.'

He sat down at the desk again. The towers were gone. He snatched up the quill.

> *'And there were gardens bright with sinuous rills.*
> *Where blossomed many an incense- bearing tree;*
> *And here were forests ancient as the hills,*
> *Enfolding sunny spots of greenery.*
> *But——'*

It was hard, at first, to identify the source of the noise. He had travelled broadly, but his experience of landslips was scant. He got up and looked out.

Most of the garden seemed to have fallen away, to allow a cascade of roaring water from the shattered conduit to hurtle down towards the sea, carrying much of Coleridge's dismembered investment with it. He could just see Alf and Esmond, waist-deep and flailing in the torrent.

He sat down again.

> *'But oh! that deep romantic chasm which slanted*
> *Down the green hill athwart a cedarn cover!*
> *A savage place! As——'*

As what? He poked about in his ruined concentration for such odd shards of dream as might perhaps remain.

Nothing stood up from the dust; but he was a poet, still.

> '*A savage place! As holy and enchanted*
> *As e'er beneath a waning moon was haunted*
> *By——*'

There was a terrible scream from outside.

> '*By workman wailing for his demon brother!*'

He looked at it. He scratched it out.

> '*By woman wailing for her demon lover!*'

Better. Not great, but not bad.

> '*And from this chasm, with ceaseless turmoil seething,*
> *As if this earth——*'

The door burst open. Alf stood there, saturated.

'It's took our Esmond off!' he cried.

'Would you mind getting out of those trousers?' suggested Coleridge, icily. 'That is a Bokhara rug.'

Alf glared at him, but class supervened.

'Co-operism is our watchword,' he muttered, and drew off the sodden moleskins.

Coleridge glanced away, embarrassed, from the heavy woollen underwear, and escaped to his poem.

'*As if this earth in fast thick pants were breathing,*' he wrote; and plunged on, scribbling maniacally. Little of the poem now made sense, but posterity would doubtless regard its disconnection as mysterious depth. He had penned several more such lines before he grew aware of Alf's anxious voice once more cutting through.

'I can see our Esmond!' he cried, from the window. 'He's half a mile offshore hanging on to the bloody gazebo!'

Coleridge let out a strangled shriek of his own, and joined Alf at the sill. He clapped his brow.

'*The shadow of the dome of pleasure,*' he muttered, '*floated midway on the waves.*'

Alf looked at him, not unsympathetically.

'I'll put the kettle on,' he said.

Waiting for it to boil, Coleridge, all remnants of the precious dream now lost, listlessly quilled his way to the bottom of the page. It was pretty standard stuff, but at

least the last two lines, he felt, had perhaps a certain
something.

'For he on honey-dew hath fed,
And drunk the milk of Paradise.'

wrote Coleridge, and tossed his quill aside as Alf emerged
from the scullery with two mugs.

'Here,' said Alf, 'this tea taste funny to you?'

A New Chapter

A new chapter was written in the history of the Royal Hampshire Regiment this week, when HRH the Princess of Wales became the Colonel-in-Chief.   Daily Telegraph

THE ROYAL HAMPSHIRE REGIMENT

This Chapter belongs to:
My Royal Highness the Princess of Wales,
Highgrove,
Tetbury,
Gloucestershire,
GL8 8TG,
England,
Europe,
The World,
The Universe,
Space.

The Story so Far: The Regiment was invented in Ireland in 1702 during the war of the Spanish Succession, which is jolly peculiar, you would think they would have it in Spain, unless they were having the war of the Irish Succession there and there just wasn't room for *two* wars (joke, joke!), and for some reason they called it the 37th Foot, which sounds to me like a horror film!!!

After 1758, they got another battalion and they called it the 67th Foot, probably because 37th Foot had been a smash hit, e.g. *Star Wars, Superman,* and their first Colonel-in-Chief was James Wolfe who went up the Heights of Abraham afterwards and wrote Gray's Energy and I think got buried at Corunna, didn't they carry his corse about—whatever that is—for absolutely *yonks?*

One *really* tacky thing is that after the Battle of Minden everybody who walked back from the battlefield picked roses and stuck them on their hats, and now they have this yeghy cap-badge with a rose on it, it is frightfully common, why on earth they couldn't have picked a foxglove or something with a bit of *flair*, or failing that, put themselves in the hands of a decent milliner, heaven alone knows.

Anyway, absolutely tons of things happened after that, battles all over Europe and the World and so forth, only they don't seem to have picked up any more flowers or anything, Colonel Wolfe probably got *really* hacked off at everybody mooning about on the way back instead of getting on with more battles etcetera etcetera etcetera and put a stop to it, anyway you couldn't keep on sticking stuff on your hat, there's nothing worse than an overdressed infantryman, Charlie says the Welsh Guards on St David's Day look like a lot of Gyppo tarts, isn't he a *hoot*, promise you won't tell!!!!

Anyway, that's all going to change now.

REALLY THE NEW CHAPTER

One of the first things I am going to do with my Regiment is get a new band going, I have heard the band they've got now and *scream, scream, scream,* it is utterly packed with big iron instruments, it looks like some ginormous Victorian loo walking about, and everything they play is roughly nine million years old!!!!

Charlie says it would be jolly hard for them to have instruments plugged in, they would keep falling over the wires, also if they had to do an invasion somewhere, e.g. or do I mean i.e. the Falklands etcetera etcetera etcetera, the plugs might be all different sizes, I think that's jolly silly of him, that's the trouble with being married to someone three hundred years old, he is utterly oh-oh-tee (he doesn't even know that it *means* out-of-touch, that just shows you how oh-oh-tee he is!!!), they could take the thing you put on the Carmen roller plug when you're in e.g. or i.e. Venice, it turns Italian electricity into ours, and then they could all have guitars and Moogs and marvy keyboards, also little pots that make coloured smoke, the Army probably have things like that anyway, I have watched manoeuvres in Germany that time I wore the blue polka-dotted Caroline Charles with the Hackett clogs and I got this absolutely ghastly Hun muck on my heels, there goes two hundred gns I said to this fearful little wimp from the MoD, he had no inkling of what I was talking about, he just sort of gargled, they are such twerpo-

twerpos, where was I? Oh yes, in the manoeuvres they had these pots of smoke going off all over the place, utterly grey and dull and monumentally blah, it would have been an absolute doddle to have done them in greens and pinks and yellows etcetera etcetera etcetera and have the Royal Hampshire Wham! or whatever sort of emerging through the smoke, it would have been ace!!!

Actually I suppose one ought to design the uniforms before one gets the group together, I would go to Susan Backhouse or Joe Casely-Hayford or Norburg & Orsuna, just IMAGINE how fantastically fantastic it would be to waltz in and place an utterly *humungous* order, Good Morning, can I have twelve thousand of these, and fourteen thousand of those, and while I'm here I might as well take five hundred dozen of those unutterably terrific boogy bracelets, they would look amazingly knock-out on the First Battalion, and the Second Battalion could wear those rubber boas they have at Total Fashion Victims, oh God, doesn't it make you want to go to war!!!! A zillion loudspeakers absolutely blasting out some fantasmagorical Shangri-La number, e.g. or i.e. *Leader of the Pack* or something, scored is that the word, for two hundred amphibious keyboards, and my Regiment boogeying up the beach like Scritti Politti through the colour-co-ordinated smoke, and the Very lights catching their studs and bangles and nose-buttons and body-shimmer, gulp GULP!

I wonder where Tears For Fears buy their clothes?

They are absolutely baggy de baggy, they would be knockout, can you imagine what a hoot to end hoots it would be going down the lines during a regimental inspection saying, oh golly, what is it they say, saying, I know, saying Oh you absolutely horrible little man, you have pressed your own trouser, your jacket is only nine sizes too big, I can see my face in your bootcaps, you have cut your hair to shoulder length, how unutterably naff, do not pass Go do not collect two hundred pounds, you are sentenced to go away and scrape off all that peculiar brown stuff there is on the outside of potatoes!

Actually, thinking of potatoes, I suppose I shall have to go into the whole business of dins.

I have been to *n* regimental bunfights where there are eight trillion tons of really tacky silver cruets and salvers and tureens and fingerbowls and little nude bods with lamps in their heads and cutlery like garden tools, and all the crocks, I mean the flat ones in front of you not the leery ones next to you, joke, joke, are covered in crests and pictures of some old queen, e.g. or i.e. one in a crown, not the etcetera etcetera, giving a flag to some poor wally with his arm shot off, and it is all very well, only what they shove on your plate is some grisly lump of dead animal surrounded by a puddle with shrivelled parsley in it, and then some fearful nerd with a shaven head so you can see all his acne dumps about nine hundredweight of mashed potato in front of you, and twelve million peas like bullets, and you know if you eat it you will instantly put on fifty pounds and your legs will go like Perrier bottles and there will be pictures of you in *The Sun* saying IN THE CLUB AGAIN! and WHEN'S THE BIG DI? and all that ghastly blah.

It is even worse than eating at home, Charlie sitting there with leafmould poultice on his bald spot and tucking into organic potting compost and daisy wine, gosh, marriage is jolly peculiar, there is absolutely nothing in those booklets about getting on with a person who thinks the new Bryan Ferry is something for taking football commentators to Dieppe, where was I, oh, yes, Army dins, well *my* regiment is jolly well not going to have a lot of stodgies and fried stuff and lard ice cream and drinks that make you burp and your teeth rot off, *we* shall have teeny things on sticks, and sidecars and pina coladas and white ladies and Pimm's Number Zillion and Badoit with a sliver of mango in it, at least we'll *start* with that, we'll probably go on to Ménage à Trois for proper sups afterwards, if they do regiments, it'll probably mean three sittings, I shouldn't wonder.

Golly, do you suppose I'd be allowed to invade things after dins?

Wouldn't it be absolutely unbelievably incredibly fabulous to put one's regiment into tuxedos and wing-collars and patent pumps and zoom off in droves to storm Camden Palace or Peppermint Park or the Electric Roller Disco, we could abseil down the front of the Hammersmith Odeon and bung bread rolls through the windows and rush in and spray Dom Pee over everybody, we could chuck barbed wire all round Kensington Palace and force

113

everyone inside to take their make-up off, *we could nuke Mustique!!!*

I bet I could even choose my own bedtime.

THE OX ambled out of the stable, not for the first time, gazed upwards, and ambled back.

'Where is it?' said the ass.

'Bang overhead,' said the ox.

'That narrows the field a bit,' said the ass. 'It is definitely one of us.'

'Unless it is a rat,' said the ox. 'There's a lot of rats in here. It could turn out to be a rat.'

'Get off,' said the ass. 'He is never going to redeem the world with a messianic rat.'

'He works in a mysterious way,' murmured the ox.

'Mysterious, I give you,' said the ass. 'Peculiar, no.'

'They are dead clever, rats,' argued the ox.

'That is not in dispute,' said the ass. 'I never said they weren't clever. He has got more cleverness than He knows what to do with; when it comes to cleverness, He is it, what He is after in a Messiah is *presence*.'

'Have we got presence?' enquired the ox.

'We have got more presence than the rat,' snapped the ass. 'For a start, we do not scuttle. Plus, we have nice natures. The world does not want a Messiah who scuttles about nipping people on the ankle. Ask anyone.'

The ox thought about this for a while.

'I'll go and have another look at the star,' it said, finally.

'Still there?' asked the ass, when the ox ambled back.

'No question,' said the ox. 'It is about time it came down, if you want my opinion.'

'Came down?'

'Yes. It will come down, and He will get out, and He will point to one of us and say *You are the Messiah, go and redeem the world.* If He is not pointing to a rat, that is.'

The ass sniffed.

'There is no evidence He travels by star,' it said. 'As I understand it, He is what is called omnipresent. He does not have to get in a star if He wants to go somewhere.'

'You've always got an answer,' muttered the ox.

'No bad thing,' said the ass, 'in a Messiah.'

The ox looked at it.

'Just joking,' said the ass.

'Yes,' said the ox quickly, sensing an advantage. 'Yes, He may not even have decided yet, He may come down in His star and make His mind up when He sees us. He may give us an interview. He may go eeny-meeny-miny-mo.'

'Eeny-meeny-miny-mo?' said the ass. 'God?'

The ox took a heavy step towards it. Its dark bulk loomed over the ass. Breath plumed from its flared wet nostrils.

'Watch it,' cautioned the ass. 'That is just the sort of thing you are on the lookout for, if you are omnipresent. He would not take kindly to the use of force. He is not after a Messiah who knocks people about. Ask anyone.'

'All right, then, clever dick,' said the ox, 'how *will* He make known to us His mysterious unfathomable ways, i.e. who has got the job?'

The ass walked slowly across the crackling straw towards the gap in which the sharp night glittered, and raised the long nozzle of its head, sniffing.

'Informed sources say it will come in the shape of three wise asses from the East. Or,' it added quickly, 'three wise oxen, of course.'

'How about—'

'No. There was definitely nothing about three wise rats.'

'If He has not made up his mind yet,' said the ox, 'it could be one wise ass, one wise ox, and one wise rat.'

The ass turned, stared—not wholly unpityingly—at the ox, and might well have said something had not, in that instant, a voice cried out from the darkness, penetratingly.

'Anyone seen three wise sheep?'

The ass whipped round again.

A ram had materialised in the doorway.

'What?' snapped the ass.

'Three wise sheep,' repeated the ram. 'They're due here any minute now, bearing gifts.'

'Gifts?' lowed the ox.

'Yes,' said the ram, confidently. 'It is traditional, I gather. Three wise sheep come from the East, bearing gifts for the Messiah. Grass, grass, and grass, as I understand it.'

The ox and the ass stared at him.

'Messiah?' croaked the ass, when it had recovered. 'What Messiah?'

'You're looking at him,' said the ram. 'Or rather, Him. It is customary at this point to fall down and praise my name, but as my three wise sheep are still en route, we might as well hang on till they get here and I can do you all at the same time. Makes sense.'

'I don't understand,' said the ass. 'The star is hanging bang over this stable, the Messiah is either me or the ox, there are—'

'Or just possibly one of the rats,' murmured the ox.

'—there are no sheep on these premises, you are well out of order!'

The ram tutted, as only rams can.

'Never mind hanging over the stable,' it said sharply, 'we have had an angel up our field, sunshine, there is no question but that I have been singled out, it is all over bar the paperwork.'

'Hail the King of the Ewes!' cried an invisible chorus.

'See?' said the ram.

The ass and the ox peered out into the night.

'Stone me!' cried the ox. 'Who are they?'

'Ewes,' replied the ram. 'My followers. You got to have followers, if you're a Messiah. It is doubtless why He chose a sheep. It is one of the main things sheep do, follow.'

There was a long uneasy silence. Finally, the ass said:

'What did this angel say, exactly?'

'Hard to tell,' replied the ram. 'There's a hell of a wind up there and I got all this wool in my ears, but the gist was *unto a us a something something* and *follow the star,* and then he give me this Look.'

'Is that all?' said the ass.

'You had to be there,' said the ram.

The ox shrugged.

'Well, that's it, then,' it said. 'Can't say I'm sorry, it's a big responsibility redeeming mankind, never mind not liking 'em much to start with, if they're not eating you they're turning you into bloody suitcases.'

'Good point,' said the ram, nodding. 'One of the first things on my agenda will be the commandment *Love Thy Sheep*. You've no idea what it's like, having them shears running over you. I go all funny just thinking about it. My millennium will spell the end of the pullover as we know it, and not before time. Also collies. I am not having the disciples rounded up and put in pens just so's some nerd in moleskin trousers can go home with a silver cup.'

The ass cleared its throat.

'That could explain it,' it said.

'What could explain what?' enquired the ram.

'The non-arrival of your three wise sheep. You got to go through Turkey, if you're coming from the East. They are probably a gross of shish kebabs by now.'

'Careful, son,' said the ram. 'When they get here with the documents, I shall be able to do miracles, e.g. turning donkeys into frogs.'

'Possibly, possibly,' said the ass. 'However, I remain to be convinced that the Almighty would entrust the salvation of mankind to something on which mankind has been putting mint sauce all these years.'

The ram narrowed its eyes.

'Listen,' it said, 'it may interest—'

It stopped.

There were new voices beyond the open door.

They were not animal voices.

'Of course,' the loudest of the voices was saying, 'the annexe cannot be compared to the main block, it does not have a bathroom, but I think you'll find it has a sort of rustic charm, and I do not have to tell you that, at the price, you would be unlikely to—'

As the innkeeper came into the doorway, his eye fell upon the ram. Whereupon the innkeeper cursed, held up one hand to stay his customers, plunged the other into the neckfleece of the intruder, and hurled it out into the night.

'What did I tell you?' said the ass, when the innkeeper had gone out again to collect his guests. 'He should never have been here in the first place.'

'Yes,' said the ox. It knitted its thick brows. 'Still, do you reckon that whichever one of us turns out to be the Messiah ought to forgive him?'

'We'll cross that bridge when we come to it,' said the ass.

Going for Gold

It is hardly surprising that we cannot interest young people in business. What turns them on is glamour and heroes, and where can they find idols in commerce?

Investors Chronicle

ELSEWHERE, NO doubt, Mr Schickelgrüber was frantically scribbling his new autograph into review copies of *Mein Kampf;* elsewhere, one gathers, Clarence Birdseye was rapturously fingering his first frozen pea; elsewhere, perhaps, Professor Goldberger was cracking a magnum across the stern of Vitamin B; elsewhere, one assumes, Louis Armstrong was honking the first few unpolished phrases that were ultimately to become *Coal Cart Blues*.

Such trivia were no concern of mine.

In that golden summer of 1925, upon its most momentous evening, my exclusive preoccupation was a bumping pitch and, yes, a blinding light: four to get and the last man in, and out of that setting sun the fearful silhouette of the fastest school bowler in all England hurtling down upon me!

I shaped for the drive, I swung the bat, the crack threw the startled rooks from the pavilion roof—but the ball, as in some dreadful nightmare, merely rolled slowly towards mid-on, and came meekly to rest.

I hardly dared look down, nor was there need; to those who know, the feel of a bat sheared off at the splice is like no other. I stood there, clutching the willow ruins, rocked by the crowd's low groan.

And then, by some miracle, I felt a strong hand upon my trembling shoulder. I turned, and found myself staring into the unwavering Corinthian eyes of Jack Heelbar, the Apollo of the Remove. His jaw jutted, his golden forelock rode the breeze, his immaculate pinstripe put my grass-stained whites to shame.

'Jack!' I cried. 'Is it really you?'

He chuckled throatily.

'I see you need a new bat, young'un,' he said. He turned to the small figure at his side, Snelgrove of the Fourth, in his long brown warehouse-coat and clipboard. 'Norman,' he said, 'we got any of them size sixes with the wossname, treble splice, in stock?'

'Just a tick,' said Snelgrove, and scuttled off towards the dear old school. He was back in a trice, the new bat bright between his inky hands. He passed it to Jack, who passed it to me.

'Oh, Jack,' I cried, 'how can I ever—'

'Seventeen-and-six,' said Jack.

I dug in my flannels for a pound. He pocketed it.

'Plus half-a-crown handling charges,' he said. 'While I'm here,' he continued, 'I don't suppose I could interest you in a new box, tested during the recent unpleasantness on the Somme, definitely guaranteed to withstand a .303—'

'Thanks awfully, Jack,' I said warmly, 'but there remains the little business of the Match!'

'Say no more,' said Jack, and retired briskly to the boundary and his Tizer stand.

Leaving me to the last ball of the game. It flew, pitched short, rose sharply, cried out for the hook; I swung, sun-blinded, and by some miracle connected. The leather sang away, cleared the rope at the first bounce: the Match was ours!

As one man, the crowd converged upon Jack Heelbar, hefted him to their shoulders, and cheered him from the field.

None of us really knew whence Jack had come. About heroes, myths accrete, shadowing fact. Certainly, it had been his great-grandfather who had led the second charge at Balaclava and won the scrap concession by a furlong from two Argentinians on a camel, thus establishing the family's fortune. Nor could anyone doubt that it had been his maternal grandfather who had, in 1881, invented a small cast-iron souvenir with a thermometer down one side and then persuaded Gustav Eiffel to turn his thoughts to a method of promoting and marketing it. But had his paternal grandfather, Beau Heelbar, *really* joined the French Foreign Legion to discover the whereabouts of the fabled Huddersfield Ruby, acquired it by masquerading as John Hanson and promising the thief ten per cent of the victrola rights in return for using the gem to back a touring production of *Desert Song,* and in fact exchanged it with the French authorities for what he subsequently turned into the Zinderneuf Heelton?

Who could say? They were a circumspect family, as I found to my cost when I enquired of Jack's father, Lord Heelbar, on his one visit to the dear old school, whether it was true that he had obtained his peerage from Lloyd George in return for services rendered when the demands of the munitions factories during the Great War left London desperately short of virgins.

In answer, the great man fixed me with one of his fabled withering looks, set his lantern jaw, and, before I could defend myself, sold me a clapped-out 1912 Jowett.

After the run-in with his pater, I did not see Jack Heelbar again until after we had both left the dear old school, I with the dreary Victor Ludorum trophy, he with outline planning permission for twelve mock-Tudor villas to be built on the cricket pitch he had won from the Headmaster following the latter's attempt to confiscate a pack of Heelbar Ltd playing-cards portraying Theda Bara in a small asp.

In the autumn of 1927, I went up to Oxford. It was as I pushed the Jowett the last few yards over Magdalen Bridge that I became aware of a banner strung across the road: WHY LOOK A PRAT, it enquired in letters three feet high, WHEN ONLY FIVE GUINEAS BUYS YOU TWO (2) PAIRS OF OXFORD BAGS, ALTERATIONS AT COST?

Beneath it, a shimmering exemplar of the fashion he had created, stood none other than the great Jack Heelbar!

'Jack!' I cried delightedly. 'Do my eyes deceive me?'

'No,' he replied, 'it is straight up, I am a fool to myself, we are killing ourselves at these prices, but it is definitely true, plus we throw in college scarf of choice and chance to go on fabulous treasure trail and win one genuine export-reject oar to stick over mantelpiece or other fine spot.'

'How do we do it, you ask?' said Norman Snelgrove, appearing from nowhere and addressing himself to my inside leg. 'By cutting out the middleman, that's how!'

'I had no idea you were up, Jack,' I said, slipping easily from my braces.

'*And* down,' replied my hero, 'I only took a First this morning, didn't I?'

'What? But you cannot have been at Oxford for more than a week!'

'How long does it take?' said Jack. 'We do not muck about up Balliol, son! Not when you are talking five hundred firkins best old tawny port, formerly the property of Alphonse Capone, recently the subject of a US Department of Customs & Excise seizure but now gone walkabout due to dropping a few bob here and there, I trust I do not have to draw pictures?'

'I say! And what's your degree in, Jack?'

'History was it, Norman?'

'Law,' said Snelgrove.

'Law,' said Jack. 'How about a nice mortar board, what are you, 6⅞?'

For the remainder of my three years, I caught no further sight of Jack Heelbar; hardly surprising since his periodic visits to the city were fleeting—to pick up a Blue for merchandising, for example, to check the navvies' progress on his by-pass, to receive his honorary D. Phil. for services to nude bathing, and so on.

But I followed his rocketing career in the newspaper columns, from which, indeed, he seemed hardly ever to be absent. When, to take one instance at random, Jack Heelbar set off in 1928 to climb Everest a few scant years after Mallory and Irving had perished in the attempt, all the world held its breath. In the event, he stopped only fifty feet from the summit, subsequently declaring in that dashing devil-may-care way of his that he had seen no point in going on, any fool could tell it was the wrong spot for a revolving restaurant, it would cost a fortune to lay on mains drainage, never mind customers experiencing difficulty in sucking steak through an oxygen mask.

Such verve was typical, such priorities the hallmark, of a man who, informed that Lindbergh had just flown the Atlantic, merely raised one eyebrow and remarked: 'Oh, really? What movie were they showing?'

It came, thus, as no surprise to those who worshipped him that when, in 1936—having by then broken the land speed record for takeaway pizza vans, turned down Wallis

Simpson upon discovery of her overdraft, beaten Fred Perry to the production of the first designer truss, become the only man ever to buy four gold medals from Jesse Owens, and generally triumphed among the myriad other opportunities with which the 'thirties were rife—that when, as I say, the Spanish Civil War broke out in that fateful summer, Jack Heelbar should have been among the very first to pack his bag and embark.

It was there, in the tragic rubble of Barcelona, that our paths were to cross for the last time.

December, 1937, and the first cruel needles of sleet were blowing off the sea, along Las Ramblas, to chill us where we lay in our rough-prepared positions among the tumbled masonry. Franco's 75-pounders having paused briefly to cool their barrels, the eerie, unsettling silence was punctuated only by the icy suspiration of the wind and the spasmodic ping from across the little square whenever, in its sandbagged fastness protected by six white flags, two red crosses, and a large illuminated sign declaring I AM AN AMERICAN NEUTRAL in English, Spanish, and German, Ernest Hemingway's typewriter came to the end of a line.

It was thus that my war-tuned ears caught, far off, the purr of an engine. Not, for once, a Heinkel, or a Tiger, but something sleek, refined, civilised among this bleak barbarity.

As it grew louder, we dared to crane above our shallow crannies. The first I saw of it was the silver stork upon its radiator, to be followed by an immensely long fretted bonnet, moving forward on huge whitewalled wheels. A straight-twelve Hispano-Suiza, suddenly gliding among us like Scarlett O'Hara ministering to the serried stretchers of Atlanta!

It slowed; it stopped. A chauffeur slid to the basket-worked rear door, and, seconds later, an elegant primrose spat touched down gently upon that dreadful pavement.

The figure emerged complete, its handblocked fedora absorbing the sleet into its lush felt, its cashmere topcoat slung rakishly across the broad shoulders beneath, its yellow kid gloves sliding a map from its crocodile case and gently unrolling it upon the bonnet.

Even from behind the man was unmistakable!

'Jack!' I cried, not for the first time in my life.

He glanced round. I sprang from my hole, ran up, and pumped his hand. He wiped his glove, and looked at me.

'Got any of that toilet soap in stock, Norman?' he said.

The chauffeur shook his head.

'Jack!' I cried again. 'Your car! Your clothes! Are you a general, Jack? A *generalissimo*, even?'

I jabbed at the map, excitedly. He winced.

'Is there relief on the way, Jack? Are we saved?'

'Don't get the map mucky, son,' he said. 'You appear to have left some kind of speck on my proposed casino complex.'

I passed a hand across my eyes. I had been out here too long.

'Casino complex, Jack?' I muttered.

In answer, he reached into the hand-stitched recesses of his uniform and drew out a number of title-deeds.

'Know what these are?' he enquired, the dear old grin playing across his handsome features. 'Benidorm, son, Torremolinos, Tossa del Mar, you name it.'

'You've captured them?' I exclaimed.

'I've bought 'em,' replied Jack. 'Course, they're not much now, rubble mainly, you can pick 'em up for a song. No problem, mind, having 'em razed, saves no end of trouble, plus not having bloody Micks all over the shop.'

'Funny thing, war,' I said.

'Don't knock it,' said Jack, hotly. 'It's been good to me, this has. There's not a lot of entrepreneurs got an entire bloody Costa. One day, son, you will not be able to move for—'

What I should not one day be able to move for I was destined never to know. For in that instant, simultaneous with a single, distant crack, a rose of blood blossomed in the centre of those dear old features and, a moment later, the best and bravest chap that I had ever known lay lifeless at my feet.

'Oh, God!' gasped Norman Snelgrove, biting his knuckle.

I turned my head away, so that he should not see me. A grown-up fellow does not blub.

'I know, old man,' I choked, 'I know.'

'I was down for one of them bungalows,' said Norman.

And far away, beyond the town, the distant guns took up their threnody.

But Answer Came There: Nun

DRIZZLED MIDNIGHT on A41, road like black shove ha'penny board, not driving on road at all, really, driving on tyre-buffed patina of old sump-droppings, slimy rain, slick skid-shards, plus, no doubt, seasonal additives, e.g. office-vomit, spilt advocaat, blood, feel like Torvill and Dean trying out secret new routine under cover of dark, Free Style Pasa Doble With Station Wagon.

Nevertheless, pushing hard, foot perilously down, seventy-plus approaching Hendon Flyover, fly over, Brent Cross Megamarket disappearing below left, sinister-lit by orange sodium and deserted, now, of shrieking yuleshoppers, looks like cobalt-strafed Alphaville, shove on, sliding, towards checkpoint.

Or, rather, Cashpoint.

Seasonal inevitability, hurtling through night with Lloyd's Cashcard, seeking slot. Equation: *Xmas = X times mass,* where X represents amount of cash believed sufficient to get through day. Hence quotidian rhythm: every night stick in card, cash appear; every day stick out hand, cash vanish.

Am formulating this, when, aquaplaning down northern slope of flyover, car suddenly shoved sideways, as if by giant hand. Juggle back to stability, peer anxiously through wiper-sweep; it not giant hand at all, it backwash of Porsche 928 rifling past like clay pigeon, tail-lights flick round bend, gone.

Must be doing ton.

First reaction, um. Second reaction, hope to God not bound for Hendon Lloyd's Cashpoint slot, know what Porsche drivers are, flash Harry gets whim to buy emerald choker in middle of night, break baccarat bank at Crockford's, take over Richard Branson, run off with Mrs Sangster, gets to Hendon Lloyd's Cashpoint first, opens boot, takes out sacks, sticks in card, siphons entire folding wherewithal of Home Counties, where that leave me?

Tomorrow morning, knock knock knock knock, merrychristmasfromthedustmenguvnorgissafiver, not got fiver, soon got fish-heads all over lawn, front gate in bin, bin on car.

Press foot down, take bend, or some of it, see traffic light ahead, light still red, Porsche still at light, hit brake, slew, slow, stop. Porsche go *thrum-thrum-thrum,* clutch half-in, straining against torque like pedigree Exocet under starter's orders.

Struggle manfully not to turn head, despite gripping curiosity, do not wish to catch eye of hot-shoe nerd, be provoked into drag-start, leave bits going ping-bonk-tinkle all over road while Porsche saunter away.

Long light.

Resistance go flabby.

Turn head.

Stare.

Nun stare back.

Nun smile gently.

Light go green.

Nun let in clutch.

Nun become twinkling dot.

Nun?

Go off, slowly, pass Lloyd's Bank in daze; what kind of nun drive Porsche 928? What kind of nun drive Porsche 928 *like that*? Italian nun, Sister Nuvolari, close second in 1951 Mille Miglia driving V-12 Miserere for Good Works Team, still keeping hand in? Unlikely. Not in Hendon.

Accelerate in inadequate pursuit, rack brains for items of conventual wisdom, could there be Extremely Closed Orders, e.g. The Rich Clares, say, or The Little Sisters of the Loaded, charged with charitable works among distressed billionaires, dedicate lives to roaring at 200 kph between Acapulco and Cap Ferrat and Dallas in hope of pulling highrollers back from purgatorial brink, dragging jetsetting, sinners from mink sheets *in flagrante*, rapping zonked-out megastars on back of head so that coke-plugs fly from cosmetized nostrils?

Up to ninety-odd now, holding own but not gaining, see Porsche half-mile ahead go through Apex Corner like Monsignor Lauda taking Druid's, whang off up A1, bat out of heaven.

Roll through in pursuit, still got Christmas tree in back, tree fall over, reek of amputated needles, box of glass balls hit floor, go off like toytown musketry, hardly notice, could this be, sudden thought, Medical Missionary of Mary? Heard about them, stuck in head on alliterative grounds, no doubt. Dashing north with bootful of kidneys, corneas, tin legs? Could well explain speed, especially if carrying only magnum of AIDS-free plasma in England, got to crash through Jehovah's Witness roadblock at Hatfield, winding up to maximum revs down long Boreham Wood straight, then BANG! and, punching out windscreen shattered by bound *Watchtower* volumes, on to Baldock to save life of seeping Carmelite felled by plummeting vesper-bell.

Long shot, mind.

Could instead be—Jesus (sorry!), am now doing 105, strange unsettling smells coming through heatervents, still not gaining on flying nun. Further sudden thought: what happen if nun stopped by Old Bill, excuse me, Sister, is this your, just step out of, blow in, and so forth, or do nuns have special dispensation, if so why not get revolving purple light stuck on roof, Gregorian siren? Sister Kojak, have a wafer, God loves ya, baby.

Evenfurther sudden thought, what happen if self stopped by Old Bill, allo allo allo, where fire? Well, officer, there was this nun in a Porsche. . .

Nun not taking M1, nun heading on towards Welwyn, settled down to steady hundred, still see tail-lights, could it be all anchorites get one day off worldly-good-renunciation, one day to drive sportscar, hang-glide, scuba-dive, buy Telecom shares, wear sable, watch *Dynasty*, play poker, ring escort agency, shoot grouse, smoke pot, support Fulham? Is Porsche bound for some glittering sacerdotal Walpurgisnacht at distant Midlands casino, full of friars telling dirty jokes in uni-order jacuzzis and cardinals jumping out of cakes?

128

Maybe,

Maybe,

Maybe not nun's Porsche at all, maybe nun ambling down Finchley Road murmuring through rosary, looked up, saw big star over, roughly, Hoddesdon, shrieked, leapt into first unlocked car, jumped starter-leads, took off north.

Or maybe, maybe, not only not nun's Porsche, but *nun not nun*! Maybe Porsche owner bizarre fetishist, crouched down in passenger seat watching habited wife, mistress, *poule de luxe*, belting Porsche through night, owner whimpering at every gear-change, fainting ecstatically at every tail-wag, why not, was not born yesterday, been about a bit, university of life, takes all sorts; come to that, could be owner himself, why not, fatigued tycoon, snapped Cabinet Minister, spaced-out pop mogul, mad gynaecologist, tough at top, no end of stress, only way to keep going, come home of an evening, shed three-piece worsted, slip into wimple, ignite Porsche, hi-ho, Silver!

Ease back throttle; must be something like that, give up unequal struggle, glance at dash, forty unanticipated miles gone, fuel low, warning-light flicker, drop to low-thirst forty, have not passed gas-station, thus push on; five miles up road to Texaco haven, pull in, fill, walk inside, pay.

'Funny thing, had a nun in just now.'

Be still, heart.

'Nun? *Genuine* nun?'

'No question. In a Porsche. I thought, hullo.'

'You would.'

'And here's the funny part.'

The *funny* part?

'Know what she bought? Apart from petrol, that is. Know what she bought?'

'Surprise me.'

'Three foot-pumps.'

Walk out again.

Stare into moonless dark. Somewhere out there, nun with three foot-pumps rocketing north, like arrow of God.

And how was *your* day?

That Summer: A D-Day Memoir

I REMEMBER waking up early.

We all woke up early, that day, in our village. I can remember, with that almost frightening stereoscopic clarity of childhood, lying in bed, with the fresh sheets smelling of Idris and the comforting sound of the Scott's Emulsion bubbling on the hob downstairs. I was five years old, and at that age the lens is sharp and the prints do not yellow or curl or fade, the way they do in adult memory. I can remember the thunder of the planes coming over, wave after wave, and the fugitives in the loft moaning, and the parrot barking.

We did not have a dog, because all the dogs had been collected up when War broke out to be melted down into saucepans, but we had a parrot because my uncle had been on the old *Café de Paris* when it was torpedoed and Al Bowlly was killed, and he came back from Mayfair, walking up the hill to our village with most of his tuxedo shot away and the parrot on his shoulder, and the parrot was singing *We'll Meet Again,* and my mother cried, and my uncle said: 'Chin up, gel, it is always darkest before the dawn,' and my mother smiled, and blew her nose, and the parrot told her to eff off.

But that had been four years earlier, and my grandfather, who still had a steel plate in his head from the Blighty one he got at Wipers after attempting to interfere with a Flemish hitch-hiker in '24, had taught the parrot to bark and shout 'Kamerad! Kamerad!' in case Hitler invaded.

I got up and went down to breakfast, and because my mother saw to it that we never went short there was Zambuk and Rinso and piping hot Rennies, and we all tucked in while the big transports and bombers roared overhead on their way to France and my grandfather said: 'The big show is on', only we could not hear him too clearly because he had been wrapped in brown paper since 1939, the way the posters told you to be in case of blast, with his Mickey Mouse gasmask over the top of the brown paper, and he had to take his Rinso through a straw.

And my mother cried, and said: 'I wish your father were here now,' and my grandfather pulled the brown paper away from his lips and told her she was a silly cow, his father was buried in Djibouti, where would they put the coffin, he wasn't having it in his room mucking up the symmetry, and my mother said she didn't mean that, she meant *my* father, i.e. her husband, and my grandfather said she was a silly cow again, if my father came down from the loft now and they caught him he would do fifteen years.

So my mother wiped her eyes, and lit an Erasmic, and said: 'Let's all listen to the news on Radio Malt,' and we all waited for the set to warm up, and then Alvar Lidell said: 'Can I do yer now, sir?' and we all had a good laugh, especially the butcher, who stayed in my mother's bedroom on Monday nights so that we were never short of a nice piece of shin, and then Alvar Lidell said: 'No, but seriously, today Allied forces under their supreme commander Colonel Chinstrap landed in Normandy and pressed inland' and Vera Lynn came on and sang *Run, Rabbit, Run* and my grandfather broke out of his brown paper and opened a bottle of Ediswan he had been saving for the invasion, in case Hitler was partial to a small one, and my mother went out into our little allotment and danced with the man who saw to it that she always had fresh horse doings for the rhubarb so that we could all see in the dark, which infuriated the butcher who said: 'Sod this, I was in a reserved occupation for people like you, I am off up to Mrs Wilmslow at Number Fourteen, you would not believe what she will do for a couple of nice trotters.'

So there was just my grandfather and I after that, and my grandfather said: 'You'd better take that bastard his breakfast up'. He was always angry about my father getting bacon and eggs every day, also the other five men, but my father was fully entitled to bacon and eggs, being flying crew, even though he had never flown anywhere except from Biggin Hill to our village on the day he got his wings and they all bailed out and landed in our orchard and the Lancaster flew on for a bit before it came down and demolished the cottage hospital. I can remember my father and his crew creeping into our house after dark, they all wore berets and blue vests and onions round their necks, and my father said: 'Can you hide us, the silly bastards wanted us to fly to Germany, they seem to have no idea there's a war on, typical War Office cock-up, fly over Germany and you're bound to upset 'em, doesn't anyone realise what an ack-ack gun can do to a Lancaster, it's only bloody sticks and fabric, all that for bacon and eggs, I should cocoa, I was getting four pound a week in civvy street.'

I nearly made a mistake over that when the King came to our village in 1943, and we all stood along the High Street waving our flags and the King came by in his big shiny Abdulla drop-head, and he stopped and got out and we all cheered, and he was not stuck up or anything, he talked to Mr Barrett the cobbler and Old Hethers and Barker and Dobson from Kute Kandies, and then he came to me, and he said: 'Hallo, little man, have you had a busy day?' and I nodded, and he said: 'Never mind, there'll be bluebells over the White Cliffs of Dover tomorrow, just you wait and see!' and then he asked me if my daddy was in the army, and I said yes, and he said: 'What does he do, or is it very hush-hush?' and I said: 'Yes, sir, it *is* very hush-hush, he's a deserter', and the King said: 'Jolly good, jolly good, we must all do our bit, keep smiling through, I will send you a plate and a mug and a memorial scroll when this is all over', and he moved on, and got in his car, and drove off, and we all cheered again, and shouted, 'Sharp's the word for toffee!' and old Mr Eucryl who was standing next to me said: 'He's a brave man, you know, a squanderbug fell on Buckingham Palace last night, we're all in this together.'

Then we all sat down at trestle tables on the village green and the landlord came over from the Monk & Glass with foaming snoek for the men and fizzy Cherry Blossom for the children, and the butcher punched him in the mouth on account of my mother never being short of gin, and I don't know what might have happened then if a German parachutist hadn't come down in Farmer Dammarhoid's field, and there was terrible confusion, what with my grandfather hobbling up in his brown paper to surrender to him, and the parachutist trying to surrender to my grandfather, and the parrot shouting 'Kamerad! Kamerad!' and my mother fighting all the other women over the parachute and the children screaming at the parrot to get it to ask for chewing-gum in German and the parrot telling the children to eff off, and the vicar rushing off to ring the church bells to warn everyone that there was a foul-mouthed parrot at large, and my father's crew hearing the church bells in the loft and thinking that Germany had invaded and running around trying to find their disguises, only the onions were all shrivelled up by now and looked like strings of dried peas and the mice had been at their berets.

But now it was 1944, and all that was behind us, and I went up the little creaky drop-down ladder to the loft with the steaming breakfast-tray, and they were all pleased to see me, especially the navigator who touched my vest and said: 'That's nice, is it Viyella?' and the mid-upper gunner shrieked: 'Touch him again, you fickle bitch, and I'll scratch your eyes out!' but my father was very forceful, being the captain and everything, and he said: 'Do stop it, men,' and they did, and he turned to me and smiled, and said: 'We've all been out here too long,' and then he asked me what all the planes were doing overhead, and I said: 'It is D-Day, daddy, it is not the end, it is not even the beginning of the end, but it is, perhaps, the end of the beginning,' and the tail-gunner said: 'Oh, bloody wizard bloody prang, Hitler has missed the bloody bus, we are not half going to cop it, now, they'll throw the bloody key away,' but my father said: 'Hang on, don't panic, I've just has this super wheeze, here's what we do. We all put our uniforms back on, and we all go outside, and we all walk about with our parachutes hanging out and trailing, and we all look sort of, you know, dazed, and if anyone asks who we are we say our Lancaster was on the way to France with all the others when it developed engine failure, and we all bailed out!' and all the men cheered, until the tail-gunner said: 'Come off it, Deirdre, this is your village, they'll recognise you straight away, you're supposed to have been killed in 1943,' but my father just laughed the mocking laugh they all had in the RAF, then, and said: 'But I have got a beard, now; we all have.'

So they all got into their old uniforms after breakfast, and they clambered down from the loft, and they went out into the warm, sunny, soft morning, one of those mornings, one of those *English* mornings, that we do not seem, somehow, to have any more, and they wandered uncertainly down the High Street, as if badly shaken, and they were just passing Kute Kandies when my grandfather, out of his brown paper now that the invasion was on, passed by on the other side, with the parrot on his shoulder, and when the parrot saw the six airmen it suddenly started shrieking ' Kamerad! Kamerad!' and old Mr Barker and old Mr Dobson looked out of the window, and ran upstairs to get their Lewis gun, because they were both in the Home Guard.

And they set the Lewis gun up in the bay window on the first floor of Kute Kandies, and they emptied an entire belt into the six airmen,

'Bloody sharp eyes, that parrot,' said old Mr Dobson to my grandfather, as they watched the bodies being slung onto the back of Mr Andrews' liver salts truck, 'fancy spotting fifth columnists from across the street!'

'He noticed they were all wearing beards,' replied my grandfather. 'Imagine the Jerry high command not knowing that British air crew aren't permitted to wear beards!'

'It's little details like that as loses wars,' said old Mr Dobson.

Hang about

Sexy actress Fiona Kendall offered a £100 reward yesterday for a missing 200-year-old tortoise called Napoleon, which has escaped from a garden in Clapham. It has been in Fiona's family for generations. The Sun

I SHALL just stand here by this gravel-bin, for a bit. I shall observe the traffic lights. It is all a question of timing. It would be a mistake to hurtle.

It could take three minutes just to get off the kerb. You got to work forward to your centre of gravity, get your head in, pivot. The secret is in the topple. You do not want to end up on your back. Could take days.

What is irritating, what is infuriating, what really gets up the nose, is being sought by the authorities under the name of Napoleon. When one was actually christened Edmund Cartwright. Apart for anything else, there are virtually none of us left who commemorate the power loom. There is, I believe, a carp in Haslemere, and there are unsubstantiated rumours of a parrot in Doncaster, but that is the top and bottom of it. *And* I have my doubts about the parrot. Ninety years is normally top weight for a parrot. You come across a lot of parrots in my game, and I have yet to see a 1785 item.

Plus, if it *is* two hundred years old, it will not be reflecting any credit on Edmund Cartwright. It will not be much more than a chipped beak with a couple of mangy feathers dangling off of it, it will also definitely be ga-ga, you would ask it who was a pretty boy then, and it would not answer 'Edmund Cartwright! Edmund Cartwright!', it would more than likely say the first thing that came into its head, e.g. 'Give us a walnut!' or 'Piss off!', something of that order, you know parrots.

The thing about a tortoise, though I says it as shouldn't, is we do not deteriorate. We look two hundred years old when we come out of the egg. Titchy, I grant you, but still could be taken for a two-tonner. Nothing falls off us, we do not go flabby, we do not slow down, you can name us after a dear or respected one and be certain we shall carry the responsibility without unsightly deterioration.

Looks like forty seconds on the red. Hardly enough time to get into your stride. Such as it is. They ought to have tortoise crossings, little green tortoises up on the lamppost, button at the bottom, you could push the button with your conk, it does not seem too much to ask, they spend a fortune on lollipop men etcetera, they sit up all night working out Green Cross Codes and similar, fat lot of use a Green Cross Code is to one of the chelonian persuasion— look left, look right, look left again, bloody hell, there's ten minutes gone straight off, before you've even got a leg out!

It is typical.

It is like being renamed Napoleon after you have been Edmund Cartwright for a hundred and eighty years, not because there has been any drastic change in your circumstances to warrant it, e.g. you have taken to shoving one leg inside your shell, but simply because it is 1965 and nobody knows who Edmund Cartwright is any more, that is how this country honours its great sons, it is the Swinging Sixties, yegh, and it is all Chink man-made fibres in your mini-skirt, it is all cheap Commie flares flooding in from East Germany, it is the death of British cotton, it is as if the spinning jenny had never been invented, people say *Why is your tortoise called Edmund Cartwright?* and nobody knows, so instead of looking him up, *Cartwright, Edmund, inventor of power loom, 1785*, it is easier to re-launch your ancestral tortoise as Napoleon, well he was old, wasn't he, anything old will do. Never mind when I was born he was only fifteen, he was *nothing*. Not that he ended up any better from my point of view, I am now walking around as a French failure, I commemorate an exile with piles, where are we all going in this country is what I want to know, where are the standards? Unlawful substances, potholes, mucky films, riots, mistresses, blackies all over everywhere, nancy boys. Sexy actress Fiona Kendall, and I quote.

Is it any wonder I have done a runner? Is it any wonder I have had it up to here?

We have come a long way from old Jabez Kendall, 1764–1839, regular churchgoer, worked a sixty-hour week, grew his own vegetables, thatched his own roof, brewed his own beer, did it twice a month with the light off, loyal subject of His Gracious Majesty, brought me home from Wisbech Goose Fayre—in those days you could go to a goose fayre, have a slap-up dinner, pint of porter, wrestle a greasy pig, deflower a virgin, buy a tortoise, and still have change out of a groat—and when they asked him my name, he said Edmund Cartwright, and there were tears in his eyes. Nobody said *Who's Edmund Cartwright when he's at home?* What happened to patriotism?

It might be wise to wait until it gets dark; but then again, it might not. I have worked out that it would take me six minutes to cross the road, i.e. four green lights, give or take, and the point is, would the traffic stop for a tortoise, would it hell, this is 1985, it is not 1785, it is not cost-effective to stop a juggernaut for a tortoise, it makes more commercial sense to wait till you get to Milan and prise him out of your Pirellis with a bread-knife, very nice; but if I wait until let us say midnight, when there is less traffic, what less traffic there is will not be able to see me at all, or, worse, this being Clapham, there will more than likely be a race riot, I will probably get picked up and bunged at a copper, I could well get filled with Esso, *Police Transit Destroyed By Molotov Tortoise, Sexy Actress Inconsolable.*

We haven't half come downhill in this country, I speak as one who knows. You cannot put anything over on a tortoise. We may not say much, but we keep our eyes open. You do not remain in a family for generations without holding a watching brief, I am not just an heirloom. I have seen a number of top Kendalls, senior cavalry officers, inventors, JPs, one who was nearly a bishop, a couple of famed solicitors. In 1873, to give you a for instance, I nearly went on a Polar expedition, only they thought it might interfere with my internal workings. It wasn't sexy actresses, then. We had India, then, most of Africa, islands all over the place, you name it. Anyone gave us any lip, bang!

Gone green again. I suppose I could always get run over deliberately, I suppose I could make a supreme gesture, it is a far, far better thing, and so forth. But who would know? *Sexy Actress Fiona Kendall's Tortoise Napoleon Flattened By Breadvan,* As opposed to *Two-Hundred-Year-Old Edmund Cartwright Had Nothing To Live For, Walked Under Breadvan, This Is Life In 1985 Britain, See Major Analysis Inside.*

You cannot even eat the food any more. I can still taste Regency lettuce, I still dream of Victorian sprouts, the Kendalls had a kitchen garden in Rhyl during the

Peninsular War, I tell a lie, the Crimean, and you would not believe the cabbages. These days, it is like chewing your way through a bathroom cabinet. It is probably doing something untold to our innards, another century on pesticides and I shall more than likely have two heads, it will be impossible to draw them in, I shall have to choose which one stays out and cops a half-brick or a rubber bullet or a nuclear bomb or whatever it is they have got in store for 2085, very nice.

Gone green again. Long line of buses, madmen on motorbikes, be ten thousand demonstrators any minute, wadder-we-want-ten-per-cent, big boots, crunch, goodbye Edmund Cartwright, *Sexy Actress Fiona Kendall Breaks Down At Inquest*. You would think there would be an easier way of getting out of Clapham, making a new start, be different if I was a black tortoise, no doubt, just off the boat, I would probably get a council flat, I would be a community leader, I would get a grant for crossing the road, if anything ran over me the RSPCBA would torch South London as far as Sevenoaks.

Getting older. Getting harder to keep the old eyes open. And has it, after two centuries of unswerving patriotism, come to this? Hibernating by a Clapham gravel bin? Dossing down between the melon pips and the squeezed-out glue tubes?

Mind you, let us not knock it, six months oblivion is six months oblivion. You take what you can get, these days.

My Suit

Simply write an article on a subject of your choice and send it to the Spectator.

There is no restriction on subject matter, but entrants are encouraged to make full use of their own particular interests and resources. The range of subjects covered in The Spectator may provide a useful basis for ideas.

IT IS a truth universally acknowledged, that a single man in possession of a good fortune must be in want of a suit.

Of course, it all rather depends on what we mean buy a good fortune. It would be frightful to have one of those bloody self-made chain-grocery fast-food used-car-lot snot-nosed dropped-aitch fortunes where one's dreadful cork-tipped lower-middle-class shag of a father kept turning up at one's Narrow Street rooms in his vomit-coloured Rolls-Royce with its JEW 1 personalised number-plate, accompanied by one's overdressed made-up Chanel-reeking ratbag of a mother looking like a mink mammoth and cackling at one's chums through her red-slashed gold-toothed ginny mouth as if she were drumming up the wherewithal for her dago ponce.

It would have to, absolutely *have* to, be a fortune rooted in a decent provenance, preferably fifty thousand acres of grousemoor wrested from the cringing undersized ricket-boned foul-smelling mentally subnormal Scots after a particularly rigorous bit of Highland Clearance and currently mooched by flocks of dim-wit billionaire wogs with their unspeakably vulgar monogrammed crocodile gunbags and their, for all I know, hand-tooled rods in, what do they call it, fibre-glass, or some such neoplastic Yank muck.

If that is what neoplastic means, although I am not much concerned whether it does or not, I should prefer to leave such sniggering nitpicking to that slimy breed of bog-raised grammar-schooled redbrick self-styled 'professors' in their made-up Tootal bow-ties and their lime-green, is the word Hush Pussies, driving themselves around in their two-tone Jap hatchetbacks between over-paid Channel 4 'programmes' about Nigger Structuralism

139

As Perceived By The Greenham Abortionist Trotskyite Dyke Workshop Heavy Metal Co-Operative, or some such.

No, one takes one's philological credo from one's beloved Lewis Caroll, unquestionably the greatest writer who ever lived: 'When *I* use a word, it means just what I choose it to mean—neither more nor less.'

Eheu, Postume, Postume, that we had such dons with us today, instead of the hereinabovementioned brown-pay-envelope Booker-scrabbling crotchstruck semiotic slugs! To be at Christ Church in the golden ante-Beveridge years before the walls fell to the infidels, to watch Keble going up tile by tile and have the foresight to know that one day Sir John Betjeman would allow one to admire it, to take little plump-kneed girls punting on the Isis and innocently photograph them in their tight shiny silk knickers, without having to do any of those loathsome beastly things one has to try to do today if one is to stand any chance of preventing one's rich well-born wife running off with the first big monosyllabic Cockney oaf who comes to clean the windows while one is round at the *Spectator* offices, honing a comma and discussing with one's chums whether a subscription-linked competition to win one of Algy's old hankies would take the circulation into double figures.

Still, to quote the wily wop again, *Brevis esse laboro, obscurus fio.* I do not seem to have arrived yet at the matter of my new suit, and since this piece was actually commissioned as a review of the latest splendid supplement to *Crockford's Clerical Directory,* it must be, I am afraid, a matter of *à nos moutons;* an ugly Frog phrase, true, but as Lewis Caroll so scintillatingly put it in *Through The Looking-Glass,* 'Speak in French when you can't think of the English for a thing.'

I had early determined—upon the principle of *wenn es eine Freude ist das Gute zu geniessen, so ist es eine grössere das Bessere zu empfinden*—that my new suit should, of course, be no ordinary suit. I wanted no horrid drip-dry ready-to-wear *à la mode* assemblage of Nip-made fibres thrown together in the evil-smelling cellars of the Ikey Mo Natty Sweatshop Company for the greater profits of a pro prietor who would doubtless use them to burrow his Levantine way into some pillar of the English establishment by—what?—buying a vulnerable lossmaking gentleman's magazine, perhaps, and instead of upholding its time-honoured principles of liberal enlightenment, filling it rather with the hysterical *partipris* rantings of his odious little clique of propagandist cronies.

No, my suit would have to be an English suit through and through, thick as a horse-blanket, abrasive as a scrubbing-brush, heavy as a tarpaulin, the sort of suit one can properly appreciate only if one has stepped gratefully into it after a bracing monastic night upon the iron-hard military mattress of an unheated stone-flagged east-facing broken-mullioned English country house; a suit whose myriad qualities will remain ever a mystery to the smirking lightweight-clad numskulls drinking urinary foreign lager in their Servowarmed executive residences as they ogle their overbreasted lubricious wives across the unspeakable Vesta moussaka by the light of Ronson permacandles, oikishly assuming this vile advertising-propagated simulacrum to be happiness. If these poor fools but knew the joys of sitting thankfully celibate at the centre of thiry pounds of good hairy lovat tweed, scanning the letters of dear Denton Welch and chewing the tart dregs of one's home-brewed barley wine!

Turn-ups would be essential, *cela va sans dire*.

Very deep turn-ups, so that if, perchance, one were to be knocked from one's Rudge by some coal-black heroin-filled homicidal jobless Rastafarian mugger and done to death in his revolting Brixton alley, the coroner, presented with a face bashed into anonymity, would at least be able to determine from the contents of one's turn-ups that one had been a gentleman: a grain or two of Pargeter's Number 8 snuff, a few crumbs residually smeared with mildewed *patum peperium*, the greying hairs of a dear dead pointer, a steel nib, a scattering of crusted bogeys for which one had had no further use—that order of thing.

The legs themselves would naturally have to be unpressable: one would not wish to give the impression that one was some kind of area sales-manager, some kind of executive, some kind of wage-earning shitehawk with a home computer and an aluminium greenhouse and a combination-locked briefcase, some kind of Rotarian loony engaged upon 'charitable' works designed to raise betting-money for feckless Ethiopean layabouts. The trouser-legs would have to be wide and tubular, concertina-ed at the knee and roomy in the seat to allow

141

air to circulate and reduce the need for inordinate changes of underwear every week or so.

The fly would button.

Perfect trousers, in short, in which to sink into one's great-grandfather's battered leather *fauteuil,*having first affixed a horn needle into the arm of one's gramophone and placed a 78 rpm record of Peter Bull reading *James James Morrison Morrison Weatherby George Dupree* upon the turntable, and open a most splendid volume that came in for review a mere quarter-century ago, *Crockford's Clerical Directory,* to which I shall address myself next week, space and the meticulous prosopography of my new waistcoat of course permitting.

Author's note to the judges: Should this entry prove successful, one would be eternally grateful if the £2000 could be paid in notes. One is presently pursued by duns, usurers, and other such gabardined filth, and a cheque would immediately be sequestrated and doubtless used to finance some shady international conspiracy or other. These grasping swine seem quite unable to distinguish between a temporarily embarrassed gentleman and a common fraud.

The Triumph of Autumn

HALLO. SINCE the very dawn of communication and our forefathers' first crude attempts to get someone else to pay for a year's dinners, man has dreamt of coming up with a unifying shuttle with which to draw together civilisation's variegated warps, slice that theme into thirteen one-hour parts, and bugger about all over the world in company with a camera crew, a few big-busted research assistants, and a BBC credit card.

Today, at last, man has cracked the secret. It lay, as it was bound to do, not with the theme, but with man himself. Themes are no problem, there are themes all over the place—sex, roofing, democracy, acne, boats, monotheism, swimming, crockery, warfare, you name it—enabling us to compare early Melanesians, say, with everyone from gay miners to third division goalkeepers, but it takes a special sort of man to put this theme across. He has to wave his arms about a lot, not look as though he is reading his thesis off bits of paper stuck all over the Parthenon or Stonehenge, and be prepared to go everywhere in a wrinkled bush shirt to give an impression of eccentricity, academic commitment and not spending too much licence-money on dry cleaning.

I am just such a man. I stand in the proud line of Clark, Bronowski, Attenborough, Galbraith, Roberts, Forsyth, and several Burkes of one kind and another.

Tonight, in Part One, I lay out my stall.

Hallo again. This, as you can see if you know anything about Hiltons, is Java. Here, on what is now the poolside barbecue, Homo Erectus, some four hundred thousand years ago, discovered (*pokes sausage*) fire. He did not, of course, discover it lying under a rotisserie, he discovered it by heaping leaves up, probably to make a bed or god, and finding it suddenly bursting into flames. Autumn can be surprisingly warm, out here.

But not here. This is the Teutoburgerwald, and I am holding the jaw of Heidelberg Man. At about the same time as, twelve thousand miles to the east, Homo Erectus was learning to cook, this chap—he had of course a body on at the time—was suffering the first cold blast of the German autumn, necessitating a move deeper into his cave. Not easy, without a rough hand-axe to chip away the rock.

And this is what Heidelberg Man invented. I have come here to the (*bus goes past*) British Museum to show you what you can do with an axe similar to the one belonging to Heidelberg Man. This comes from their collection of early British crude tools, and if you bang it against a stone wall like this, oh. Er, British stone-age tools, of course, would break if you banged them against anything hard, because they were not designed to enlarge caves. English autumns were warmer. . .

. . . as you can see by looking at Hadrian's Wall, demarcation line between England and (*picks up bagpipes, bagpipes squeal*) Scotland. It has been up for eighteen hundred autumns, and has hardly got a mark on it. The Roman legionaries looking out of this embrasure, incidentally, would probably be eating something very similar to this spaghetti of mine, though without, of course, this very acceptable little 1976 . . .

. . . Pomerol. Here, in Bordeaux, autumn is the time of (*barefoot man in beret jumps into vat*) the vendange, when they harvest the grapes which have been grown in these rolling fields since before the founding of Sumerian civilisation.

What, do you suppose, is this strange triangle, weathered now by the Mesopotamian sun (*glances up, Iranian Mig 27 screams overhead, until brought down by Iraqi Exocet*) but still etched deeply enough into its host lintel for those of us familiar with Cuneiform to be able to read it, some five thousand years after that long-dead hand first chiselled it? Yes, of course, it is the Sumerian for 'autumn'! For it was here, upon this great alluvial plain watered by the Tigris and the Euphrates, that literacy began.

And not only (*walks through Foyles, struggles briefly with mad Swedish assistant*) literacy. This (*reappears in middle of*

Euphrates, doing breast-stroke) was also the site of the Garden of Eden and thus the cradle of the Judaeo-Christian tradition, in which the Fall plays so large a part, and in which it is symbolised by the autumn leaves which Adam and Eve snatched up to hide their nakedness when shame entered the world (*swims to shore, where topless Samantha Fox is eating an apple*). To the Chinese, however. . .

. . . the year 3500 BC—in other words, almost the precise moment at which our Sumerian stonemason was inscribing autumn over his front door—means the date upon which the first of the Sage Kings began that civilising process which led, in a few short centuries, to the remarkable Ch'in Dynasty, dominated by Shih Hwang Ti, who built this Great Wall upon which I am now standing! Funny thing, history. The Chinese legionaires looking out of this embrasure, incidentally, would probably be eating something very similar to this crispy duck of mine, though without, of course, this very acceptable little 1976. . .

. . . Piesporter Goldtröpfchen Spätauslese. Here it was (*camera pulls back to show narrator pacing deck of paddle-steamer*) in the lush Rheinland, that, scarcely three thousand years after Shih Hwang Ti was declaring the Great Wall open, Johann Wolfgang von Goethe was penning perhaps the greatest words ever used by a German to describe a citrus harvest (*interior of Albert Hall, male voice choir of the Metropolitan Police*):

> KENNST DU DAS LAND WO DIE ZITRONEN BLÜHN?
> IN DUNKLEN LAUB DIE GOLD-ORANGEN GLÜHN,
> EIN SANFTER WIND VOM BLAUEN HIMMEL WEHT,
> DIE MYRTLE STILL UND HOCH DER LORBEER STEHT—

and yet (*removes helmet, tucks it under arm, and descends through humming policemen*) Goethe himself never actually witnessed autumn in a lemon grove. This supreme act of the poetic imagination was achieved without visiting

Israel, or

Florida, or

Come to that, Spain. Where (*kills bull*), among other places, the secret of powered flight remained naught but a pervasive dream, until that fateful autumn day in 1903, when, in a field beside the rolling Atlantic Ocean at Kittyhawk in. . .

. . . North Carolina, Orville and Wilbur Wright began the series of heart-stopping runs which was to lead, eventually, to. . .

. . . Concorde. It was here, just a little more of the Beluga, thank you, it was here, forty thousand feet below us, that on the crisp autumn morning of September 21, 1327, the hapless King Edward II was cruelly murdered in the grim dungeons of. . .

. . . Berkeley Castle (*footsteps echo down damp lichen-hung stone passages, flickering candle throws dramatic light upward, prominating nostrils*). A homosexual, yes, but a plucky and unabashed one, whose notorious long-standing affair with Piers Gaveston, had it not taken place in the less-enlightened fourteenth century but, instead, in present-day. . .

. . . San Francisco, would certainly not have resulted in his being bayoneted where, as we historians say, the moon don't shine. It may, by the way, interest you to know that just a few miles down the coast from where I am eating this excellent lobster gumbo, Walter Huston was born, father of John and, most important of all, given the theme to which we shall be addressing ourselves over the next three months, the man who made famous *this* little number! (*camera pulls back, showing table-companion to be Liza Minelli, who removes a lobster claw from her mouth, and sings*):

Well, it's a long, long time,
From May to November,
And the days grow short
As you reach September.

And the days dwindle down,
To a precious few. . .

(*Singing grows fainter as Fisherman's Wharf restaurant simultaneously dwindles with the plucking of narrator from his chair by helicopter winch. Narrator dangles ever higher over San Francisco Bay, as Earth's curvature becomes more apparent.*)

This, then, is our world. And over the next twelve fascinating weeks, we shall, together, be looking at the enormous influence that autumn has, for umpteen thousands of years, brought to bear upon it. Nothing will be left out, from the birth of Thomas Aquinas to the rise of the big bands, from the Otto cycle to oven-ready courgettes, from origami to Macdonald Hobley, from. . .

(Fade, roll credits, plug book)

Her Upstairs

God is not a male deity and there is a case for addressing God as 'Our Mother', according to a report published yesterday by the Church of Scotland.   The Times

Dear Mr Coren:

I am a first-time writer but a long-time reader, I hope you will excuse this approaching you out of the blue but I do not know where to turn and I have always understood you to be straight with people, esp. women, you are virile but humane and will not make cheap jokes etc. about God not being able to find Her lipstick, that is not your way. This Church of Scotland announcement could do big things for the Women's Movement, is it true She made the world in six days?

Alice Cole (Ms), Yarmouth

Dear Ms Cole:

Thank you for putting your trust in me, you are absolutely right about my taking this seriously, it is not every day that one wakes up to find that God has changed sex, even in Scotland.

Strictly speaking, no, She did not make the world in six days. Not everything in the Bible is to be taken literally, as I'm sure you know. But, and here's the point, She *got* it done. She knew this absolutely wonderful little firm round the corner, and they did all the basic labouring, dividing the waters which were under the firmament from the waters which were above the firmament, and so on, after She told them where the firmament had to go. She said, *Let there be light,* and lo! they put it in.

She did all the carpets and curtains Herself, though.

Dear Mr Coren:

I have a boutique and a husband and two small children and there always has to be a hot meal on the table, never mind if the Sales are on, even, or we are awaiting deliveries from Belgium or similar. What I want to know is, how did God manage to combine a successful career with raising a family, i.e. Her only begotten Son?

Shirley Roth (Ltd.), Barnes

Dear Limited Shirley:

A good point, and we have to face the fact that she did *not* actually raise Her only begotten Son. She employed a couple. It is probably the only way open for a working Mum.

Of course, being God, She was able to take delegation even further than most working Mums in that She also got the couple to have the only begotten Son *for* Her, thus enabling Her to carry on working right through the pregnancy. It is a neat trick, but not generally available on the NHS; I understand, however, that Mr Patrick Steptoe is able to offer something along similar lines, at a price, although you would have to select your couple with great care. Pick a middle-class pair, for example, and He might end up as a barrister and that would be the last you saw of Him, you can earn £80,000 a year as a QC, it beats wandering around in sandals and touching lepers for a living.

Dear Mr Coren:

All right, okay, great, big deal, terrif, God was a woman, is that supposed to make everything nice, you condescending eunuch bastard?

Just what kind of a woman was She? Why didn't She send an only begotten Daughter, tell me that, I would have thought that if you were trying to save the world, I mean do you have any idea *how men have screwed up this planet, the last thing you'd send is a, a, yegh!*

Tell me that, you Nazi pig.

Malvolia Greenham, Cockfosters

Dear Malvolia:

While I agree absolutely that women by their very natures are much nicer people and that an only begotten Daughter would have been absolutely ideal in some ways, in others it would have been rather tricky.

In early AD, a woman just could not go around on her own, she would not get served in pubs or be allowed to play golf unescorted, in short she would not have access to those places you had to get into if you wanted to redeem personkind. The only course would have been to arrange for an only begotten Son-in-Law, possibly even only begotten Grandchildren, and not only would the teleological conundra have become virtually insuperable, the only begotten Daughter would have had a terrible time at public meetings, with women asking questions about combining homecare and careers instead of listening to useful homilies.

She would almost certainly have had to appoint an only begotten Chairman to keep order, and half his time would have been spent with nonsense like *We have a question from a Galilean listener who would like to run over that recipe again, is it five loaves and two fishes, or two loaves and. . .*

I trust you take my point, Malvolia. Times were not then as they are now. I'm convinced the second coming will be entirely female, if it's any consolation.

Dear Mr Coren:

I am having great difficulty in coming to terms with this new proposition, given some of the, well it has to be said, quite beastly things that God has done. I mean, I realise of course that they had to be done, one has to take a firm hand with some people, look at the miners, but one or two divine actions do seem to me to smack of the male touch. For example, did She really slay all the Egyptian first-born? It seems extraordinary behaviour, even for a zealous and almighty Mum!

Lavinia Gribling, Poole

Dear Lady Gribling:

You are of course perfectly correct, and many eminent Scottish theologians are even now examining the Bible closely for what are obviously glaring mistranslations.

As far as *Exodus* is concerned, I am happy to be able to inform you that what She actually did was insist that the first-born tidy their rooms up and stop picking their nose. Provided they did that, they would be allowed to come downstairs and watch the plague of boils. Well, pimples, really.

Dear Mr Coren:

Sorry, sorry, sorry, I am just an 'ordinary' housewife and not, is the word 'into', feminism and so forth, my hubbie Gerard would be furious if he thought I was bothering a busy man like you with my 'nonsense', but I feel sure God understands about us 'little people', doesn't She? After all, Her eye is on the sparrow, am I correct?

Anyway, I was very excited about God being a lady, and all I want to know, on behalf of all of us who are beginning to 'spread' a bit, is did She have Her own special secret for staying slim? Is it a question of 'what you eat' or 'how you eat'? Or did She take exercise, if so what form, are there those stationary bicycle efforts 'up there'?

Germaine Hodge, Bromley

Dear Mrs Hodge:

Goodness me this is a bit of a poser! How often you 'ordinary' folk turn out to be not ordinary at all and ask just the sort of tricky question that puts us so-called experts right on the spot!

The fact is that now we are pretty certain that God is not, as was previously believed, an old man with a long white beard, what is She? Clearly, not an old woman with a long white beard, but beyond that we do not have a great deal to go on, except that She made us in Her image, so we all look a *bit* like Her, and it's quite clear that couldn't be possible if She were not fairly average, probably about five feet five, slightly swarthy skin (although of course free from blemish of any description), and with manageable hair, which She does Herself.

As to build, this really is unknown territory, one can hardly begin to conjecture: She could be an absolute knockout, She could be more sort of comfy and maternal, but whatever She is, that is the way She stays, since She does not eat anything, being divine, and does not take exercise as you and I would recognise it, being omnipresent. I suppose we shall all just have to wait until that glorious day when we at last gaze upon Her face and are not dazzled.

I hope that answers your question.

Bridge In The Afternoon

Twenty-five years ago, at the age of sixty-one, Ernest Hemingway took his own life. It is not easy to think of him in old age, passing the time as old men do.   Atlantic Monthly

AROUND NOON, I went down to the club to cut the sandwiches.

There was nobody in the hall, so I did not have to feel uncomfortable about being a young one. Sometimes, it is not easy to be a young one walking into a bridge club in the afternoon when there are old ones about. Many of the old ones are very old ones, and a few of them are practically dead ones, and when they hobble out of the card room on the way to the bath room and then they stay in the bath room a very long time, the way very old ones do, you get to feel uneasy being a young one.

You get so you wish you had wrinkles and a pot belly and cataracts and trouble down there where the very old ones have trouble, especially when it is time to bang on the door and shout:

'Are you all right in there, old one?'

And the old one shouts:

'Why should I not be all right in here?'

And you say:

'I am only doing my duty, old one.'

And the old one screams:

'I obscenity in your duty! I obscenity in your mother's duty, and your father's duty!'

I walked down the hall, and out back to the little kitchen, and I opened the big refrigerator and I took out the sliced bread and the big German knife with the black bone handle, and I put the slices into piles of four and began to cut off the crusts, so that the old ones would not choke or break their upper plates or spend two hours chewing the same sandwich. This is partly because I care about the old ones, but partly because I care about the furniture, and when an old one has to open the bidding and cannot say 'one club' without blowing wet crumbs and little pieces of tuna all over the green baize, you know you are in for a long night with the brush and the pan and the solvent, and maybe you will not get home until three o'clock and your woman is asleep, and there is nothing to do but lie awake and stare at the car headlamps making patterns on the ceiling.

When I finished cutting the sandwiches, I did the thing with the cling-wrap, and I put them back into the refrigerator, and I shook a few peanuts into little glass bowls, and I took the bowls into the card room, and I set them down on the tables.

The old one was sitting at a table. He was gazing out the window, and doing the fancy thing with the shuffle which all the great *internazionali* do. I leaned forward, but with much respect, and took some of the cards out of his trouser turn-ups and one off his hat. The rest I left on the floor.

The old one looked up at me.

'Cheap cards,' he said. 'How do they expect a man to shuffle with cheap cards? What are they making cards out of, these days? These are not man's cards.'

'Perhaps it is something they put in up at the factory,' I said.

The old one picked at a dried egg-flake on his lapel.

'When I made the seven spades against Manaleto and Ortega,' he said, 'the cards were like silk. They were like some part of a woman that they have found out how to print on. Each time I played a card from my hand, the crowd gasped.'

'They were a knowing crowd,' I said.

'They had *aficion*,' said the old one. 'That is the way it is at the Pamplona Rotary.'

'I have heard of the seven spades against Manaleto and Ortega,' I said.

'Who has not?' The old one pulled out a big red-spotted bandanna and blew his nose fiercely, if inaccurately. 'Manaleto and Ortega were from the hard region up around Escarte Dolo, where they breed the fighting bridge-players. The fighting bridge-player is to the domestic bridge-player as the wolf is to the dog.' He wrapped one big liver-spotted hand around the other and cracked a knuckle. It was like a walnut going. 'A domestic bridge-player may be evil-tempered and vicious as a dog may be evil-tempered and vicious, but he will never have the speed, and the courage, and the peculiar brain of the fighting bridge-player, any more than the dog will have the sinews of the wolf, or his cunning, or his savagery. They are bred from a strain that comes down in descent from the wild whist-players that have ranged over the Peninsula for centuries.'

'It could not have been easy, the grand slam with the spades,' I said.

'It was 1969, I was but seventy summers, I had *cojones,* but no, it was not easy,' nodded the old one. 'When my partner, the great Ginsberg, opened two clubs and Manaleto overcalled three hearts, I knew we were in for a fight.'

'It can be terrible, the *intervencion,*' I said.

The old one shrugged.

'It is a *convencion,*' he said. 'A man must respect the *convenciones.* Without them, the game is nothing. Man is nothing.'

'You might as well play canasta,' I said.

'Spoken like a true one, young one,' said the old one. 'You might as well play kaluki with the women.'

He took off his hat, and fanned himself with it, for the day was hot, the way it can be in those regions when the boiler is old and the valve is stuck, and he looked at me, very hard.

'Tell me,' he said, 'have you, yourself, *aficion?*'

I looked away.

'I am green,' I replied, 'but I will progress. At present, I play the Strong No-trump and the Preferred Minor.'

The old one laughed, a cracked noise in his soup-flecked beard.

'Forgive me, young one. There is much to learn. You could not go up against Manaleto and Ortega with such equipment. You would sustain a wound. You could go five tricks light, and you would not be able to walk again where the big ones walk. One day, if I am spared, I shall show you how to play the big ones, when to use the Neapolitan Club and the Schenken Transfer, I shall tell you about Fischbein and the. . .'

There was a ring at the door.

'Forgive me, old one,' I said, 'that will be the other ones.'

The old one spat.

'Send not for whom . . .' he said, and tailed off. His forehead furrowed, like the shore at Capodimonte under

155

the ebb. '*Ask* not for whom?' he murmured. 'Send not to *know* for whom . . . ?'

I went across the card room and into the hall and I opened the big front door with the coloured glass panels, and North and East shuffled into the club, a little in front of South, who had caught his Zimmer frame in the door-scraper and was screaming at it.

I helped North out of his topcoat. It was like shelling one of those big boiled crabs they do at Astispumante, only without the garlic.

'Is the old bastard in, kitchen one?' said North.

'Please do not call me kitchen one,' I said.

'He is a proud one, for a kitchen one,' said East. He pulled off his left galosh, and fell over. 'That is the way they are, these days.'

I looked at him.

'I am a *novillero*,' I said. I lifted South out of his frame. His bones were like a bird's. 'Today, I cut the sandwiches and play the Strong No-trump, but tomorrow I shall wear the suit of three pieces and play the Neapolitan Club.'

'Ha!' cried North. 'He has been talking to the old bastard. He has been getting advice from West.'

'Nobody plays the Neapolitan Club any more, young one,' said South.

They hobbled into the card room, and they grunted at West, but he did not look up, nor when they sat down. He just pushed the cards across, with one of those clean, spare movements the great ones have, and said:

'Cut.'

I went out, then, and back again to the kitchen, and I began the thing with the cocoa, so that it would have time to cool down after it had heated up and they would not have to blow on it and get froth all over one another. I thought a lot about West while I stirred the lumps out, of the way it is to be eighty-six years old and to have come so far from Oak Park, Illinois, to be blown up on the Italian front, and to sit in the hotel in Madrid while the falangists laid down the big barrage from their 88's so that all the whiskey bottles broke, and to write all the books and win all the prizes, and how the best of all was to make the seven spades grand slam doubled and vulnerable against Manaleto and Ortega.

I was still thinking all this when I heard the cry from the

156

card room, and I ran, then, because it could have been East's angina or South's gallstones or North's prostate, but it was none of these.

'What happened?' I said, after I had put my ear to West's waistcoat and heard nothing but the ticking of his big half-hunter.

'The old bastard bid seven spades,' said North, 'and went six off.'

'It killed him,' I said. I looked out of the window. 'It was the *ignominia*. It was the dishonour.'

'It cost me seventeen hundred goddam points,' said East. 'The old bastard. We were doubled and vulnerable.'

I looked away from the window, and back at the table. The cards were spilled out, like blood.

'It was the contract he played against Manaleto and Ortega,' I said. 'But he was younger, then.'

'I do not believe he ever played against Manaleto and Ortega,' said North.

I looked into North's eyes after that, and he looked into mine, but he was the first to blink. I picked up the great one, then, and I carried him out to the kitchen, and I laid him on the table, the way they always lay the great ones out in a side room so that those with *aficion* can file past with their hats in their hands.

Then I went back into the card room, and I sat down opposite East in the vacant chair that was still warm, and I gathered the cards together, carefully, and when I had done that, I looked up, because I was ready, now.

'Deal,' I said.

SHEATH-BURSTING ROMANCE!!!

BRUTE!

MALCOLM BENNETT & AIDAN HUGHES

BRUTE!
Colossal, work-hardened men! Wild untameable women!
Savage, unbridled passion! Raw and erotic tales of
gut-wrenching drama and suspense!!

BRUTE!
Romance, cruelty and religion! Sport, crime and agriculture!
Horror, western and football!!

BRUTE!
The cult comic of the 80s now unleashed in paperback!

'**Unmatched in contemporary British comic art**'
CITY LIMITS

'**Tough and dirty**' **THE FACE**

'**Graphic, gruesome and hilarious**' **BLITZ**

'**In future all novels will be written like this**' **TIME OUT**

0 7221 1565 2   CULT/GENERAL FICTION   £1.95

A THOROUGHLY LEWD COLLECTION OF EXCEEDINGLY RUDE RHYMES!!

BAWDY Limericks

Ribald, ingenious, hilariously blue – this side-splitting selection of bawdy limericks will have you reeling with riotous laughter and mirth-filled merriment. There's Adam complacently stroking his madam . . . Irene who made an offering quite obscene . . . Hyde who fell down a privy and died . . . the young fellow of Kent who had a peculiar bent . . . the brainy professor named Zed who dreamed of a buxom co-ed . . . and many, many more!

0 7221 1297 1   HUMOUR   £1.95

A selection of bestsellers from Sphere

FICTION

THE PRINCESS OF POOR STREET	Emma Blair	£2.99 ☐
WANDERLUST	Danielle Steel	£3.50 ☐
LADY OF HAY	Barbara Erskine	£3.95 ☐
BIRTHRIGHT	Joseph Amiel	£3.50 ☐
THE SECRETS OF HARRY BRIGHT	Joseph Wambaugh	£2.95 ☐

FILM AND TV TIE-IN

BLACK FOREST CLINIC	Peter Heim	£2.99 ☐
INTIMATE CONTACT	Jacqueline Osborne	£2.50 ☐
BEST OF BRITISH	Maurice Sellar	£8.95 ☐
SEX WITH PAULA YATES	Paula Yates	£2.95 ☐
RAW DEAL	Walter Wager	£2.50 ☐

NON-FICTION

NEXT TO A LETTER FROM HOME: THE GLENN MILLER STORY	Geoffrey Butcher	£4.99 ☐
AS TIME GOES BY: THE LIFE OF INGRID BERGMAN	Laurence Leamer	£3.95 ☐
BOTHAM	Don Mosey	£3.50 ☐
SOLDIERS	John Keegan & Richard Holmes	£5.95 ☐
URI GELLER'S FORTUNE SECRETS	Uri Geller	£2.50 ☐

All Sphere books are available at your local bookshop or newsagent, or can be ordered direct from the publisher. Just tick the titles you want and fill in the form below.

Name _____

Address _____

_____

Write to Sphere Books, Cash Sales Department, P.O. Box 11, Falmouth, Cornwall TR10 9EN

Please enclose a cheque or postal order to the value of the cover price plus:

UK: 60p for the first book, 25p for the second book and 15p for each additional book ordered to a maximum charge of £1.90.

OVERSEAS & EIRE: £1.25 for the first book, 75p for the second book and 28p for each subsequent title ordered.

BFPO: 60p for the first book, 25p for the second book plus 15p per copy for the next 7 books, thereafter 9p per book.

Sphere Books reserve the right to show new retail prices on covers which may differ from those previously advertised in the text elsewhere, and to increase postal rates in accordance with the P.O.